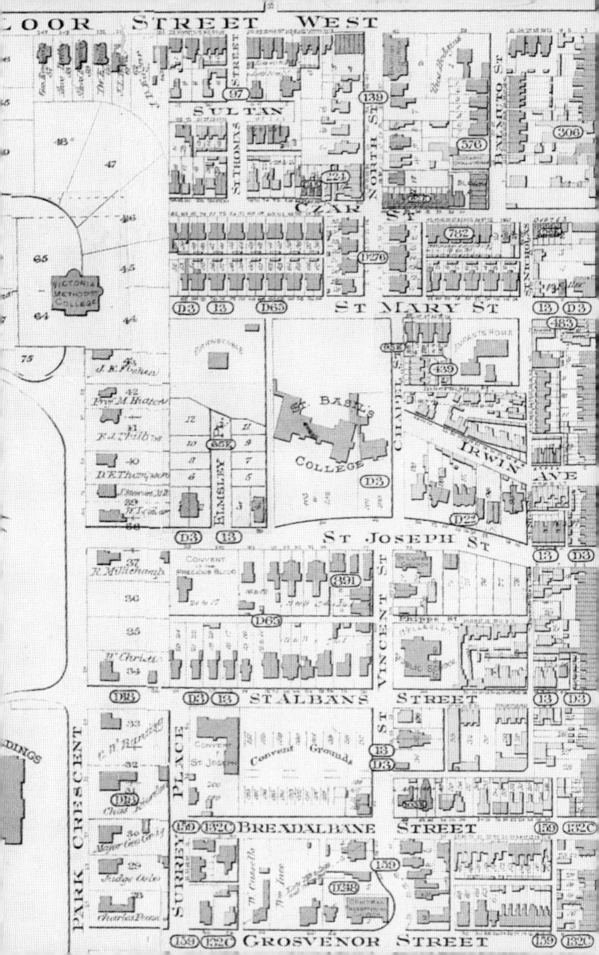

TORONTO STREET NAMES

AN ILLUSTRATED GUIDE TO THEIR ORIGINS

A FIREFLY BOOK

Published by Firefly Books Ltd. 2000

First Printing

Canadian Cataloguing in Publication Data

Wise, Leonard
  Toronto street names: an illustrated guide to their origins

ISBN 1-55209-386-7

1. Street names – Ontario – Toronto – History. 2. Toronto (Ont.) – History.
I. Gould, Allan, 1944- . II. Title.

FC3097.67.W57 2000	971.3'541	C00-931267-6
F1059.5.T6875A2 2000		

Published in Canada in 2000 by
Firefly Books Ltd.
3680 Victoria Park Avenue
Willowdale, Ontario, Canada   M2H 3K1

Editor and Project Manager: Charis Cotter
Photo Research: Vivien Leong and Karen Lathe
Research: Scott Mitchell
Design by Interrobang Graphic Design Inc.
Printed and bound in Canada by Friesens, Altona, Manitoba

The Publisher acknowledges the financial support of the Government of Canada through the Book Publishing Industry Development Program for its publishing activities.

TORONTO STREET NAMES

AN ILLUSTRATED GUIDE TO THEIR ORIGINS

LEONARD WISE & ALLAN GOULD

FIREFLY BOOKS

Acknowledgements

We could not have written this book without the invaluable contributions made by the many people who worked on it with us. We would like to thank everyone at Firefly who gave their time and energy. Of the many reference books we consulted, we would like to give particular notice to Eric Arthur's *No Mean City*, William Dendy's *Lost Toronto*, Linda Lundell's *The Estates of Old Toronto* and Don Ritchie's *North Toronto*. Other excellent resources were Mike Filey's many informative books about Toronto and Jeanne Hopkins' fascinating newspaper articles. Finally, we would like to thank our editor, Charis Cotter, who integrated the information from various sources and helped shape the street entries, making a much valued contribution to the character of this book.

Introduction

Street names provide a highly visible record of Toronto's history. Each day as we walk, cycle or drive through the city, scenes from history flash by. At Yonge we see the Queen's Rangers cutting through the bush when the town of York was founded in 1794. On Davenport a column of Natives follows an ancient route from the Don River to the Humber. Jarvis recalls a tragic duel when a headstrong 18-year-old met his death. Roncesvalles shows us future residents of Toronto fighting in Spain against Napoleon's troops. At Montgomery we see rebels with pitchforks confronting the armed militia during the Rebellion of 1837. At the Gardiner Expressway we observe an early Metro Council meeting dominated by the first chairman, Fred Gardiner.

Toronto's rich history has been intricately woven into the names of our streets. From the early 10-block settlement on the lakefront laid out by Governor Simcoe in 1793 to the sprawling megacity of 2000, Toronto has spread inexorably into the surrounding countryside, levelling ravines and paving over streams. And every step of development is reflected in our street names.

This book offers a fascinating glimpse into the stories behind the names of our streets. Without knowing their histories, some names may appear irrelevant. Why call a street Nina? Or Mercer? But when you know that Nina Wells' mother died giving birth to her, and her heartbroken father moved his family back to England and died himself two years later, the street name takes on its true meaning. And when you discover that Andrew Mercer died rich without a will and his scheming housekeeper failed to win his estate, which was then used to establish a grim Victorian institution to reform fallen women, you can never pass that street again without the vision of its history rising to greet you.

Each street name opens a window into the city's past. York's first inhabitants named streets to commemorate relatives and friends or towns and villages left far behind in England: Willcocks, St. George, Cottingham. Retired soldiers like Walter O'Hara recalled their military glory days with names of famous battles: Sorauren, Roncesvalles. The British influence abounds in streets that bear the names of government officials or royalty: Gladstone, Clarendon, Alberta, George, Adelaide, Melbourne, Pembroke. And the gracious estates that once lay outside the city proper now echo in downtown streets: Bellevue, Dupont, Chestnut Park, Rose Hill, Rathnelly, Glen Edyth, Rusholme, Dovercourt.

The citizens who lived here left their names throughout the city: brewers (Bloore, Copeland, Severn), politicians (D'Arcy Magee, Borden, Laurier), architects (Sheard, Howard), philanthropists and educators (Massey, Ryerson), axe makers (Shepard) and innkeepers (Steeles).

The streets presented in this book have been chosen for their interest and historical significance. They make up just a small fraction of the hundreds of streets within Toronto. The book has been designed with careful cross-references and a detailed index so you can dip in and out and enjoy an intriguing ramble through the streets of the city. Along the way you will make the acquaintance of many of the colourful and determined characters who shaped the city of Toronto.

How To Use This Book

To help you locate the streets on a map, each street has been given a location. Smaller streets have been given the nearest cross-streets (Dunn Ave.: Dufferin/King). Main streets have been given a starting and ending point and their position between other main streets (Yonge St.: Queen's Quay to Steeles between Bayview and Bathurst). The boundaries used are Lake Ontario to Steeles and Pickering to Mississauga. If a street extends beyond the borders of the city of Toronto, for the purposes of this book its ending point is still noted as the boundary (Dufferin St. goes past Steeles but its northernmost Toronto boundary has been given as Steeles).

Cross-references to related streets are given where applicable.
Spelling has evolved over the years: Bloore became Bloor, Sherborne became Sherbourne, Copeland became Copland. For clarity's sake, streets are referred to by their current names: Queen rather than Lot, Bay rather than Terauley, Broadview rather than Mill Rd.

Every effort has been made to discover the true origin of a street's name, but when sources differ, the alternatives have been provided.

ABBEY LANE

Sherbourne/Front
See **PETER ST.**

ADMIRAL ROAD

Avenue Rd./Bloor   Admiral Augustus Warren Baldwin (1776–1866) was a younger brother of Dr. William Warren Baldwin, who built Spadina House and laid out Spadina Ave. Augustus Baldwin joined the navy as a young man, initially as a victim of a press gang. Press gangs were groups of sailors who kidnapped able young men and carried them off to sea, thus forcing them to join the navy. However, his position was quickly regularized after he made himself known to his admiral and then obtained his father's permission.

Russell Hill, Admiral Augustus Baldwin's home, stood on what is now Glen Edyth Place. Circa 1870.

Augustus enjoyed a long career in the navy and eventually was made an admiral himself. He settled in Canada in 1817, buying the lot next to his brother's from Elizabeth Russell. There he built a two-storey Regency house and named it Russell Hill, after the Russells and his birthplace near Cork, Ireland. The house stood close to his brother's home, Spadina, on what is now Glen Edyth Place. Augustus Baldwin served on Upper Canada's Executive Council from 1836 to 1841. He died in 1866, and his widow moved out of the house soon after. The house eventually burned down. Admiral Rd. was originally part of his estate, as was Russell Hill Rd. Part of his estate was sold to Samuel Nordheimer, who built Glen Edyth. See **BALDWIN ST., GLEN EDYTH DR., PETER ST., SPADINA AVE.**

AGINCOURT DRIVE

Midland/Sheppard   John Hill was a merchant who in the 1850s repeatedly tried to get a post office for his little community northeast of the city of Toronto. Finally he approached his friend Joseph-Élie Thibaudeau (1822–78), who was a member of the government in the Legislative Assembly of Canada. Thibaudeau agreed to get him a post office if Hill would give it a French name. Hill complied, but the French name he chose was that of a famous English victory. Agincourt, France, was the site of a battle in 1415 when the French were defeated by the English army led by Henry V. Thibaudeau was no doubt surprised at Hill's choice, but thinking it an attractive-sounding name, he endorsed it. The village of Agincourt was eventually absorbed into the city of Scarborough, but Agincourt Dr. remains as a reminder of John Hill's sense of humour.

ALBERT STREET

Queen/Yonge   Albert St. was named in honour of Albert of Saxe-Coburg-Gotha (1819–61), who married his first cousin Queen Victoria (1819–1901) in 1840. In 1857 he was given the title Prince Consort. Albert was a German alien and therefore unpopular with the English people at first. Later, however, Prince Albert was widely admired for his good character, devotion to his wife and concern for public affairs. He died of typhoid in 1861 and was deeply mourned by the Queen, who built the Albert Memorial and Albert Hall in his honour. See **QUEEN ST.**

ALBERTA AVENUE

Davenport/Ossington   This street was probably named after the province of Alberta, which was named after Queen Victoria's fourth daughter, Princess Louise Caroline Alberta (1848–1939). She was married to Douglas Sutherland Campbell, the Marquis of Lorne and the 9th Duke of Argyll (1845–1914), who served as Canada's Governor General from 1878 to 1883. Princess Louise was the first British princess to live in Ottawa's Rideau Hall, the seat of the Governor General in Canada. She and her husband founded the Royal Society of Canada as well as the Royal Canadian Academy, both dedicated to improving the state of culture in the country. After they returned to England in the early 1880s, Princess Louise continued to be involved in socially conscious projects, such as better education for women. She wrote many articles on these subjects for a number of magazines under a pen name. Her husband died in 1914, but she continued her activity in the community and eventually became an accomplished sculptor. See **QUEEN ST.**

ALBERT FRANCK PLACE

Front/Jarvis   Born in Holland, Albert Franck (1899–1973) was the long-distance swimming champion of Belgium in 1924. He immigrated to Montreal in 1926, where he coached swimming at the central YMCA, and then settled in Toronto in the late 1920s. After the Second World War, he and his wife, Florence Vale, moved to a house at 90 Gerrard St. West, where Franck set up shop as a picture restorer and hanger and began to display his own paintings. The house became a focal point for young artists, including Oscar Cahen, Ray Mead, Harold Town and Walter Yarwood. Town later described the Gerrard St. neighbourhood and its eclectic inhabitants as "the only real Bohemia Toronto has ever known" (Town, 19). Franck found his inspiration in the old houses and back lanes of Toronto's shabbier neighbourhoods and exhibited his work in one-man shows and group exhibitions at various Toronto galleries during the 1950s and 60s. Before moving to his new home on Hazelton Ave. in 1954, Franck held the first two Unaffiliated Artists Exhibitions at his Gerrard St. shop in 1950 and 1951 to showcase the work of artists who were not members of the official art societies of the day. In November 1973, the Art Gallery of Ontario presented a retrospective

TRL T 30773

Albert Franck found his inspiration in Toronto streetscapes.

exhibition entitled "A Tribute to Albert Franck." Albert Franck Place was named in a public competition held in 1979 to designate several new streets in the St. Lawrence Neighbourhood housing development. See **HENRY LANE TERRACE, DOUVILLE COURT, LONGBOAT AVE., PORT-NEUF COURT, SCADDING AVE.**

ALEXANDER STREET

Carlton/Yonge   Alexander Wood (1772–1844) was a Scottish merchant who owned a store on the northwest corner of King and Frederick streets. He was quite successful and was good friends with some of the most influential people in the town of York. He became a magistrate, but his reputation was damaged by a homosexual scandal in 1810, and he returned to Scotland. Wood admitted that he had inspected the genitals of several young men, but claimed that this was to check for scratches in connection with a rape case he was investigating. Wood came back to York in 1812 and took up the threads of his life. Eventually he managed to live down his reputation, by virtue of the loyalty of his powerful friends, his business success, and his ongoing devotion to public service (he served on several commissions and continued his work as a magistrate). In 1826 he purchased 25 acres north of Carlton St., including the area where Alexander St. and Wood St. now run.

ALHAMBRA STREET

Bloor/Roncesvalles   This street was named by Colonel Walter O'Hara after the famous palace and fortress in Granada in southern Spain, which was built by the Moors between 1248 and 1354. The name is a corruption of the Arabic "Al Qal'a al-Hamrá," which means "the red castle," referring to the red clay used in its construction. The palace occupies 35 acres on a high ridge overlooking the city and is considered one of the finest examples of Moorish architecture, although much of it was destroyed by conquerors and natural disasters. The beauty and exotic nature of the Alhambra's architecture and the rugged romanticism of its natural setting have given rise to many legends and stories over the years, some of them based in fact. The word itself still conjures up the image of a remote castle in an old tale, where daring exploits and fabulous adventures once took place. See **O'HARA AVE.**

AMELIA STREET

Parliament/Wellesley   Amelia Playter was the granddaughter of Captain George Playter, a Loyalist who settled with his family in York in 1796 and was granted a sizeable lot north and east of Yonge St. Amelia married John Scadding Jr., the son of John Scadding, another early settler in Toronto. After her husband died in 1845, Amelia remarried and lived on Amelia St. The street may have been named after her, but it also may have commemorated Princess Amelia (d. 1786), the youngest daughter of King George II (b. 1683, r. 1727–60) and Caroline of Anspach (d. 1737). See **PLAYTER BLVD., SCADDING AVE.**

ANDERSON AVENUE

Eglinton/Yonge   This street was probably named after Thomas Winslow Anderson (1809–95), a watchmaker who owned a farm on north Yonge St. He opened his watchmaking shop in 1832 at the corner of Yonge and Richmond. He was involved in the famous Rebellion of 1837 and escaped to the United States. In 1840 he was pardoned and came back to Toronto. He lived on his farm until his death in 1895.

ANNAN DRIVE

Birchmount/St. Clair   The origin of this name is not clear. There is a town in Scotland named Annan, situated on the Annan River, and several Scottish immigrants to Canada had the surname Annan. There might be a connection to one of the estates of Dr. Herbert Bruce, the Lieutenant Governor of Ontario from 1932 to 1937, who had two different homes named Annandale: one at Bayview and Lawrence from 1920 until 1930, and another at Steeles and Bayview from 1930 until 1932. He named his homes after his hero, Robert Bruce (b. 1274, r. 1306–29), Lord of Annandale, King of Scotland and hero of the Scottish War of Independence, who won the decisive battle of Bannockburn in 1314. See **BRUCE PARK AVE.**

ARDWOLD GATE

Bathurst/Davenport   Timothy Eaton (1834–1907), founder of the late, lamented department store chain Eaton's, had three sons and three daughters. The youngest son was John Craig Eaton (1876–1922), who married Flora McCrae (1881–1970) in 1901 and was knighted in 1915. Sir John and Lady Flora built their home, named Ardwold (Gaelic for "high green hill"), on the north side of Davenport Rd. Completed in 1911, Ardwold was designed by Alexander Frank Wickson, who was inspired by country houses built in Ireland and Britain in the 17th century. Ardwold provided its owners with a splendid view of Lake Ontario and the burgeoning downtown area. Situated just north of present-day Casa Loma, the Eaton home had 50 rooms, including 14 bathrooms, a conservatory, a swimming pool, and a cupola on the roof for viewing the setting sun. There was also a hospital on the third floor. Unfortunately, Ardwold was demolished in 1936. Ardwold Gate was originally the drive that led to the mansion.

TRL T 11208

Ardwold, the home of Sir John Craig Eaton and Lady Flora Eaton, in 1922.

ARJAY CRESCENT

Bayview/Lawrence   Robert John Fleming (1854–1925), known as RJ ("Arjay"), left school before his teens to work selling wood and coal for a local merchant. During this early period of his life, Fleming lived on a farm near Eglinton and Don Mills. He did very well as a salesman and in 1886 ran successfully for alderman. Fleming served as mayor of the city of Toronto in 1892–93 and again in 1896–97. Known as "the People's Bob," he resigned from public office in 1904 and worked for the Toronto Railway Company. When it came time to name the new street, his son, G.O. Fleming, who had owned the land in this area, requested that it be named after his father.

A road-repair crew works on the wide and fashionable Jarvis St. in 1899.

CTA RG 8 Series 14 Vol. 1 Item 23

ARMOURY STREET

University/Dundas   A series of armouries were constructed in the 1880s and 1890s across Canada by the federal Department of Public Works under the direction of Thomas Fuller. The Toronto Armouries were built in 1893 just north of Osgoode Hall. The building was huge: the drill hall measured 280 feet by 125 feet and was 72 feet from the floor to the ceiling. Bowling alleys and rifle ranges filled up the enormous basement. Towers marked each corner and side entrances. Like an impregnable medieval fortress, the Armouries were an imposing presence, with red bricks accented by Kingston limestone. The Regimental Band and Bugles, the band for the Queen's Own Rifles, played for their monthly regimental parades here. The Armouries were headquarters for Toronto's militia regiments until they were finally torn down in 1963. Today the Moss Park Armouries (far less impressive!) may be found at Queen and Jarvis streets.

ASPENWOOD DRIVE

Leslie/Steeles Two bachelor brothers named John and William Duncan farmed in the early 19th century on a property just south of present-day Steeles Ave., running between Leslie and Woodbine. They purchased the 200-acre farm from Dr. William Baldwin in 1830 for $300 and called it Aspenwood. Both brothers supported the rebel leader William Lyon Mackenzie. Indeed, they even let their home be used as a hideout during the Rebellion of 1837. Peter Matthews (who was later hanged for his part in the uprising) and several other rebels were found hiding there. See **BALDWIN ST., LOUNT ST.**

ASQUITH AVENUE

Bloor/Yonge Herbert Henry Asquith (1852–1928), 1st Earl of Oxford and Asquith, was Prime Minister of Great Britain from 1908 to 1916. He led the country through a tumultuous period, guiding Parliament through major constitutional change, barely avoiding a major civil war in Ireland and struggling through the first two years of a devastating war. Asquith's style of politics was based on reason, loyalty and patience, and although these qualities served him well throughout much of his career, the British public lost their faith in him as a leader during the first two years of the First World War. He did not appear to have the decisiveness and flexibility needed to deal with the crisis, and he was replaced by David Lloyd George. See **LLOYD GEORGE AVE.**

Before 1915 Asquith Ave. was known as Bismarck Ave., named after the German Chancellor Otto Edward Leopold von Bismarck (1815–98), known as the Iron Chancellor. He provoked both the Austro-Prussian War (1866) and the Franco-Prussian War (1870–71), and effectively created the German empire. To show his appreciation of the honour bestowed on him by the city of Toronto, he wrote a letter of thanks, which was read out at the council meeting on May 21, 1883. "In reply to your kind letter of March 27th, permit me to state that I feel myself highly honored by the Resolution of the City

Council naming one of their streets Bismarck Avenue … " However, times change. In 1915, near the beginning of the First World War, property owners on the street petitioned City Council to change the name to Asquith, and City Council obliged. Several other streets and towns with German names were changed at the same time (for example, Berlin, Ontario, changed its name to Kitchener in 1916), reflecting public opinion during the war in which more Canadian lives were lost than in any other conflict (59,769).

AUGUSTA AVENUE

College/Spadina
See **BALDWIN ST.**

AUSTIN CRESCENT
AUSTIN TERRACE

Bathurst/Davenport   James Austin (1813–97) came to Canada as a youth from Ireland in 1829. Apprenticed as a printer to William Lyon Mackenzie (the future mayor, rebel and grandfather of William Lyon Mackenzie King, Prime Minister of Canada, 1920–30 and 1935–48), he had to leave the country after the 1837 Rebellion because of his political affiliations. He returned in 1843 and began to make his fortune, first by investing in a grocery business, and then by moving into finance. Austin developed into a shrewd and successful financier who held several important positions in the city's growing business milieu. He was one of the founders of the Dominion Bank in 1871, which eventually merged with the Bank of Toronto in 1955 to become the Toronto Dominion Bank. Austin introduced the concept of branch banking to Toronto by establishing a second branch on Queen St. West to complement its main office on King St. East, a few blocks away. He served as the bank's first president from 1871 to 1879. He was also instrumental in starting the Queen City Fire Insurance Company in 1871, serving as vice-president and president. Austin was elected to the board of directors of the Consumer's Gas Company in 1859, and served as president from 1874 until his death in 1897. In 1865 Austin purchased the Baldwin house, Spadina, and rebuilt it on a grand scale, with a 42-foot drawing room and crystal gas-lighting fixtures. The house has been preserved as a museum. See **BALDWIN ST., SPADINA AVE.**

BABY POINT CRESCENT
BABY POINT ROAD
BABY POINT TERRACE

Bloor/Jane The Baby Point area of Toronto marks a historic site on the banks of the Humber River where an Iroquois village, Taiaiagon, once stood. This village marked the southern end of the Toronto Carrying Place, the portage that linked Lake Ontario to Lake Simcoe, Georgian Bay, and points west via the Holland River. The Baby (pronounced "babby") family was a French family that settled in the Detroit area and was involved in the fur trade for many years. James Baby (1763–1833) was born in Detroit and educated in Quebec. Because his family was loyal to the British, Governor Simcoe appointed him to the Executive and Legislative councils in 1792 to represent French interests. In 1793 he was made a judge. Over the years, Baby bought and was granted many thousands of acres in Upper Canada, including the area now named after him. During the War of 1812, Baby commanded the 1st Kent Militia. His home in Sandwich (now Windsor) was pillaged by the invading United States Army in 1813. Baby settled in York in 1815, where he was appointed Inspector General. A Roman Catholic, he aligned himself with

NAC C 014253

Fort Rouillé was built in 1749 on the shoreline of Lake Ontario, where the CNE grounds are today.

other conservatives in the ruling classes in York and eventually became "one of the most influential members of the Family Compact" (Scadding, 256). He enjoyed many government appointments over the years (115 in all) and was well respected. When he died, shops and offices were closed to honour him.

TRL T 30689

Drawing of houses to be constructed on Baby Point Rd., 1913.

BAGOT COURT

Bathurst/Lawrence   Sir Charles Bagot (1781–1843) was a British politician and diplomat who served briefly as Governor General of Canada from 1842 to 1843. Born in Ruguley, England, and educated at Rugby and Oxford, Bagot was elected to the British Parliament in 1807. He distinguished himself first as Under-Secretary of State for Foreign Affairs, and then as minister to France and the United States, and ambassador to Russia and The Netherlands. In 1817, Bagot negotiated a crucial deal with the American Secretary of State Richard Rush (the Rush-Bagot Agreement), which established disarmament on the Great Lakes and Lake Champlain. In his brief tenure as Governor

General, before the illness that led to his death cut short his term, he drew great support from the French by inviting their leader, Louis-Hippolyte LaFontaine, to join the Executive Council. The Conservatives were outraged at these efforts at diplomacy and his attempts to include the French were abandoned by his successor. See **ROBERT ST.**

BALDWIN STREET

College/Spadina   Baldwin Street commemorates William Warren Baldwin (1775–1844), who was an influential figure in the early history of the town of York. He practised both law and medicine and served as a judge and a member of the Legislative Council. When the Americans invaded York in April 1813, Dr. Baldwin cared for the wounded. Born in Knockmore, Ireland, and trained as a doctor, Baldwin came to Canada with his father, Robert Baldwin, in 1798

The first Spadina House was built by Dr. William Baldwin in 1818 and destroyed by fire in 1835.

and began to study law. To supplement his income, he taught boys in his landlord's house, and in 1803 he married one of his landlord's daughters, Phoebe Willcocks. She inherited her father's lot in 1813 and part of her cousin Elizabeth Russell's considerable estate in 1822. The Baldwins built a house at the top of the hill overlooking the lake, just beside where Casa Loma stands today. They called it Spadina (then pronounced "Spadeena"), which came from a Native word, "espadinong," meaning hill. Dr. Baldwin laid out Spadina Ave. in 1836 and planted imported chestnut trees on each side. At 132 feet across, it was one of the city's widest streets, stretching from Bloor St. to just south of Queen St. At that time several streets in the area were named after members of the Baldwin family and family connections. Baldwin was named after William Baldwin; Phoebe St. and Willcocks St. after his wife and her family; Robert St. after his son; Augusta Ave. and Sullivan St. after his son's wife, Augusta Elizabeth Sullivan; St. George St. after his friend Laurent Quetton St. George and Russell St. after Elizabeth Russell. Baldwin practised law in York and served as a member of the Legislative Assembly for two terms. A well-respected and prominent member of York society, he held firm political beliefs that he passed on to his son, Robert Baldwin (1804–58), who became a key figure in the Reform Movement. William Baldwin supported responsible government in the English model and the civil and religious liberties protected by the British constitution. These issues became the focus of the Reform Movement and the struggle for responsible government led to the Rebellion of 1837. See **ADMIRAL RD., PETER ST., ROBERT ST., SPADINA AVE., ST. GEORGE ST.**

TRL T 31037

Dr. William Baldwin was an influential and respected figure in York society.

BALLIOL STREET

Davisville/Yonge Balliol St. and Merton St. are believed to have been named sometime between 1873 and 1880 by a Professor Pike, who was a chemistry teacher at the University of Toronto and lived in the area. He named the streets after two famous colleges of Oxford University in England. In the Middle Ages, groups of students rented houses together and shared expenses. These organizations were known as "houses of scholars." Eventually they gained legal status and became colleges. Balliol College was founded in 1263 by John de Baliol. The Baliols were a royal English family that had come to live in England with William the Conqueror. John married a Scottish princess and his son John (b. 1249, r. 1292–96) and grandson Edward (r. 1332), were Kings of Scotland. Merton College was founded in

Looking north on Yonge St. in 1915, with the Belt Line Railway bridge and Balliol St. in the background.

1264 by Walter de Merton. Murder-mystery fans will recognize Balliol as the college where Lord Peter Wimsey, the aristocratic detective from Dorothy L. Sayers' books, distinguished himself as a scholar and cricket player.

BANTING AVENUE

Dufferin/Sheppard   This street was probably named after Frederick Grant Banting (1891–1941), one of the men who developed the use of insulin to fight diabetes. Raised on a family farm near Alliston, Ontario, about an hour's drive north of Toronto, he graduated from the University of Toronto in medicine in 1916 and served as a medical officer in France during the First World War. He was decorated after being wounded in action, spent a year completing his training as an orthopedic surgeon, and then practised medicine in London, Ontario. Banting did not have a brilliant academic record (he failed his first year in arts at the University of Toronto and then switched to medicine), nor was he a well-trained medical research specialist. Yet late in 1920 he came up

with the idea of isolating insulin to fight one of the great killers of the time –
diabetes. The University of Toronto supported his proposal, and in May 1921
the insulin project began, directed by Professor John James Rickard MacLeod
(1876–1935). Charles Herbert Best (1899–1978), then 22 years old, served as
an assistant. Dr. James Bertram Collip (1892–1965), a biochemist, also joined
the team. They successfully isolated insulin, and this discovery made the dif-
ference between life and death for millions of sufferers of diabetes. In 1923
Banting and MacLeod were jointly awarded the Nobel Prize for Medicine.
Banting gave half of the money he won to his young assistant, Dr. Best. He
received many honours during his lifetime, including an annuity for life from
the federal government, a life membership in the Canadian Club, and a
knighthood in 1934. Banting was also appointed Canada's first professor of
medical research at the University of Toronto. For a time he was considered
the most famous man in Canada. In 1941 he was killed in a plane crash on a
flight to England.

Arthur S. Goss NAC PA 123481

Dr. Frederick Banting revolutionized the treatment of diabetes by
isolating insulin in the 1920s.

BASEBALL PLACE

Broadview/Queen   Baseball Place was once the major entrance to the Toronto Baseball Grounds, home of Toronto's first professional baseball team. The Toronto Maple Leafs of the International League started playing in 1885. Over the years they enjoyed huge success, winning the pennant 12 times and sending many famous players, coaches and managers on to the major leagues (Sparky Anderson, Bubba Morton, Pat Scantlebury, Reggie Smith, Ozzie Virgil). Throughout their history they played in various stadiums. The stadium at the Toronto Baseball Grounds near the southwest corner of Queen and Broadview, not far from the mouth of the Don River, was built in 1886. It seated 2,000 and became known as Sunlight Park, due to its proximity to the Sunlight Soap Works. In 1897 a new stadium was built at Hanlan's Point Amusement Park. It burned down in 1909, but was rebuilt, and in 1914 Babe Ruth, then a rookie pitcher for the Providence Grays, hit his first professional home run there. The ball landed in the Toronto Bay. By 1926 the Maple Leafs were playing at the Maple Leaf Stadium at the foot of Bathurst St., south of Lake Shore Blvd., and here they remained until 1967, when the team went bankrupt. Professional baseball returned to Toronto in 1977 when the Toronto Blue Jays began to play at Exhibition Stadium, where they stayed until SkyDome opened in 1989. See **BLUE JAYS WAY, STADIUM RD.**

BATHURST STREET

Bathurst Quay to Steeles between Yonge and Dufferin   Henry, the 3rd Earl of Bathurst (1762–1834), held the position of Secretary of War for the Colonies from 1812 to 1827, during the reign of George IV of England (1820–30). One of his responsibilities was to organize the migration of settlers from the British Isles to Canada after the War of 1812. In 1827, the Earl of Bathurst granted the charter to King's College (now the University of Toronto), Toronto's first university. He never visited Canada. Originally Bathurst St. stretched from Government Wharf in the harbour to Queen St. (Lot). Supplies for the garrison were received at that wharf, which was renamed Queens' Wharf when Victoria ascended to the throne in 1837. For many years, Bathurst St. north of Queen St. was known as Crookshank's Lane, after the Honourable George Crookshank (1773–1859). Crookshank, who was the Receiver General for a time, was a member of a Loyalist family that moved up from New York state in 1796. He owned 300 acres between Queen and Bloor and Lippincott and Manning. Crookshank's Lane was a semi-private lane connecting his farm to the town of York. It would not be until 1870 that the name of that stretch was formally changed to Bathurst St. Above Bloor, Bathurst was only a muddy trail leading to Seaton Village and Bracondale, which were annexed by Toronto in 1888 and 1909, respectively.

A cigar store on the west side of Bathurst St. just north of Dundas, circa 1935.

BAY STREET

Queen's Quay to Davenport between Yonge and University   In 1797 Bay St. was named when the town of York extended its boundaries for the first time. It ran from the bay to Lot St. (Queen). Dr. Henry Scadding wrote: "Old inhabitants say that Bay Street was at first Bear Street, and that it was popularly so called from a noted chase given to a bear out of the adjoining wood on the north, which to escape from its pursuers, made for the water along this route"

(Scadding, 222). North of Queen, Bay St. was linked to Teraulay St., which continued north to College St. Teraulay St. was named after Teraulay Cottage, the home of James Macaulay (1759–1822), who acquired a large piece of property in the area in 1797. The Church of the Holy Trinity, just west of the Eaton Centre, now occupies the spot where Teraulay Cottage once stood. By 1924 Teraulay St. and several other streets north of College to Davenport were renamed as part of Bay St.

CTA/TTC Fonds Series 71 Item 3629

Looking north to City Hall while shoppers, snow and traffic clog Bay St. on Christmas Eve, 1924.

BAYVIEW AVENUE

Front to Steeles between Leslie and Yonge   Governor Simcoe and his Queen's Rangers surveyed the first concession road east of Yonge St. in 1796. For years it was little more than a track through the woods. Eventually the road was named Bayview, after the home of James Stanley McLean (1876–1954), the founder of Canada Packers. His mansion was designed by the architect Eric Arthur (who wrote the excellent history of Toronto and its architectural development, *No Mean City*) and completed in 1931. McLean's 50-acre estate ran north and south of Lawrence Ave., east of Bayview. Just before James McLean's widow died in 1967, her property was expropriated by the city of North York to be part of the Sunnybrook Health Science Centre. The house was renamed McLean House, and it can now be rented for occasions such as engagement parties, weddings, bar mitzvahs and high school graduations, with the proceeds going to medical research.

Bayview Ave. north of Eglinton was a muddy country road in 1910.

BEATRICE STREET

Dundas/Ossington

See **GORE VALE AVE.**

BEDFORD PARK AVENUE

Avenue Rd./Lawrence   Bedford Park was the name of a small village clustered around Yonge and Lawrence. The Bedford Park Hotel was a tavern just south of Fairlawn, built in 1873. William Gordon Ellis and his brother, Philip Ellis, were jewellers whose business, Birks-Ellis-Ryrie, eventually became Birks Jewellers. In 1889 they bought a piece of property bounded by Bathurst to the west, Yonge on the east, Woburn to the north and Lawrence on the south. They planned to develop the property as a factory town, with a factory and hundreds of small houses for its employees. However, when the villages of Bedford Park, Davisville and Eglinton were amalgamated into the town of North Toronto in 1890, the new town council nixed the factory but passed the housing proposal. The streets were laid out and eventually the houses were built.

BELLEVUE AVENUE

College/Spadina   This street was named after the first house in the area, Belle Vue, the home of George Taylor Denison (1783–1853), son of Captain John Denison (1757–1824). George was born in England and came to Upper Canada at the age of eight. In December 1806 he married Esther Borden Lippincott, who owned 3,000 acres in Richmond Hill. Denison served with the militia in the War of 1812 and the Rebellion of 1837. He helped build Dundas St. from the Garrison to Lambton Mills. In 1815 he purchased 156 acres from Peter Russell, extending from Queen to Bloor and from Lippincott to Augusta. He built Belle Vue at the northeast corner of Bellevue Ave. at Denison Square. This Georgian home was surrounded by his farmlands, orchards, woods and ravine. Denison accumulated much of his wealth through his marriages; he was married four times. At his death in 1853, he was the owner of 556 acres of Toronto, and one of its wealthiest citizens. Belle Vue was demolished in 1890. See **BROOKFIELD ST., DENISON AVE., DOVERCOURT RD., HEYDON PARK RD., LIPPINCOTT ST., RUSHOLME RD.**

BENVENUTO PLACE

Avenue Rd./St. Clair Real estate developer Simeon Henan Janes (1843–1913) made his fortune buying large tracts of land, subdividing them, and then reselling them at a great profit. He bought up all the property between Avenue Rd. and Bathurst, and Dupont and Bloor (now known as the Annex) and laid out the streets. He was particularly fierce about driveways and refused to include any in his plans, designating back laneways instead for stables, garbage collection and tradesmen. Many of these laneways disappeared as the area was built up, and today's residents can blame the lack of parking in the area directly on Simeon Janes. Janes built his home on the west side of Avenue Rd., south of Edmund Ave., between 1888 and 1890, using the American architect A. Page Brown. Benvenuto means "welcome" in Italian. The house was a magnificent Norman structure, with grey stone walls capped by red Spanish roof tiles. The interior decoration was carefully planned, with tapestries, antiques, sculptures and murals. A stone wall encircled the estate and an intricate wrought-iron gate stood at the end of the driveway. In 1897 the house was sold to Sir William Mackenzie, and by 1927 it was vacant,

TRL T 11350

Benvenuto's Norman grandeur was capped with red Spanish roof tiles. Circa 1890.

surrounded by apartment buildings. In 1932 the house was demolished. All that remains of this once glorious structure is the stone wall on Avenue Rd.

BERKELEY STREET

King/Parliament   This street was originally called Parliament St. because in 1797 the first Parliament buildings in York were built on a spot just south of where Berkeley and Front streets intersect today. It eventually became known as Berkeley St., named after one of the first houses in York, which was situated on the southwest corner of King and Berkeley. This house, built in 1794, belonged to Major John Small (1746–1831), who was the Clerk of the Executive Council of Upper Canada. Small named the house after the little town in Gloucestershire, England, where he came from. Major Small was known as a hospitable fellow who used to call out to friends on the street to come in for a fine dinner. His dining table was large enough to accommodate 50 guests, and often did. He is remembered for a duel he fought in 1800 with Attorney General John White, his neighbour. There were bad feelings between their wives, and White spread rumours about Mrs. Small. Major

TRL T 11510

The hospitable John Small built Berkeley in 1794. Circa 1885.

Small challenged White to a duel, shot him, and White died of his injuries. At his request his remains were buried under a summer house at the back of his lot, a spot where he used to sit and study. Small was tried for murder and acquitted. After that, things were difficult for the Smalls socially for quite some time, but eventually they were accepted again in York society. He grew quite wealthy, and his sons prospered. The house was demolished in 1925. See **PARLIAMENT ST., COXWELL AVE., SMALL ST.**

BERRYMAN STREET

Bay/Davenport   Dr. Charles Berryman was Dean of the Medical College, which was located on this street, and he was also the jail surgeon and a practising doctor in Yorkville. He was active in the incorporation of the village of Yorkville in 1853, and he lived in a house on the east side of Yonge St., just below Bloor.

BETHUNE BOULEVARD

Markham/Kingston   John Bethune (1751–1815), born in Scotland, was a Presbyterian minister who served as a chaplain for the 84th Regiment (the Royal Highland Emigrants) in the British army against the American rebels in 1776. He continued with the regiment in Halifax, New York, and eventually, Montreal. After demobilization he established a small Presbyterian congregation in Montreal and then settled in Williamstown in Glengarry County, Upper Canada. There in 1787 he founded St. Andrew's Church, the first Presbyterian church in Upper Canada. Presbyterians were a minority in the Anglican-dominated Upper Canada and the Catholic-dominated Lower Canada. He protested the Marriage Act of 1793, which allowed only Anglican clergy or Justices of the Peace to perform the marriage ceremony. His sons, John and Alexander Neil, attended John Strachan's school in Cornwall and eventually became Anglican ministers. Alexander Neil became the second bishop of Toronto (Strachan was the first). Norman Bethune, the Canadian doctor who would become a hero of the Chinese Communist revolution, was one of John Bethune's descendants.

BEVERLEY STREET

Dundas/Spadina There is some doubt whether Beverley St. was named after Sir John Beverley Robinson (1791–1863), Solicitor General, Attorney General, and Chief Justice of Upper Canada, or his son, the Honourable John Beverley Robinson (1820–96), who had a long political career capped by his appointment as Lieutenant Governor of Ontario from 1880 to 1887. They both lived for a time in the house called "Beverley" on the southeast corner of Queen and John. It is quite possible that the nearby street was named after the famous house, rather than either of the Robinsons. The family name "Beverley" that they both carried came from a house owned by Sir John's great-uncle on the Hudson River, which was called Beverley House. The Robinsons were Loyalists who moved to Canada from the United States after the Revolutionary War in 1776. John was close friends with John Strachan and an influential member of the Family Compact. It was Robinson who sentenced Samuel Lount and Peter Matthews to hang after the Rebellion in 1837. Beverley House was the scene of many important meetings and society dinners, and

The elegant Beverley House stood for almost 100 years near the southeast corner of Queen and John.

TRL T 11468

served as the vice-regal residence for a time when Robinson was out of the country and the Lieutenant Governor needed a place to live. Robinson was the unwilling subject of a great scandal. Anne Powell, the daughter of the Chief Justice at the time, W.D. Powell, was infatuated with Robinson for years and pursued him, even when he was married. Eventually she followed him across the ocean and was drowned. See **LOUNT ST.**

BINSCARTH ROAD

Mount Pleasant/St. Clair   William Bain Scarth was born in 1837 in Scotland. His family descended from the Scarths of Binscarth, in the Orkney Islands. He was a land commissioner who, along with his brother, James Lendrum Scarth, managed the Toronto office of a company formed in Glasgow, Scotland, in 1880: the Scottish Ontario and Manitoba Land Company Ltd. They developed land in what is now Rosedale. William Scarth built the first North Glen Road bridge, at his own expense, to give access to the land the company was developing. The first street on which lots were sold was named Binscarth Rd. The company also was responsible for a farm for pure-bred stock in Manitoba, near where the town of Binscarth is today. See **HIGHLAND AVE.**

BIRCHCLIFF AVENUE

Birchmount/Kingston   Scarborough, about seven miles east of Toronto, was for a time a summer retreat for many city dwellers. The Scarborough Bluffs, a series of dramatic cliffs along the lake, were lined with graceful birch trees. In 1878 people made the trip out from the city to have picnics and enjoy the views and the fresh air, and from the 1880s well into the 20th century, many built cottages and summer homes there. Birch Cliff was the name of one of these homes, and in 1907 when the first post office was established in the area, it took the name Birch Cliff for the postal district. To get to Birch Cliff from the city, people used horses and buggies at first, then in the 1890s bicycles became popular. In 1898 the electric railway made its appearance. The Hunt Club (1895) and a golf course (1910) were built in the neighbourhood.

BISHOP AVENUE

Yonge/Finch   Bishop Ave was probably named after the most decorated pilot of the First World War, William Avery Bishop (1894–1956). Billy Bishop was sent to France during the first year of that war, initially as a cavalry officer. He soon moved from earth-bound horses to sky-bound airplanes, joining Britain's Royal Flying Corps in 1915. He was a very gifted and very, very lucky pilot, the top-scoring Allied ace of the First World War. By the end of the war Billy Bishop had downed 72 enemy aircraft. He was awarded the Distinguished Service Order, the Military Cross and the Victoria Cross – the first Canadian airman to earn the latter. During the Second World War, Billy Bishop was an honorary air marshal in the RCAF, and, like many a good Canadian, he died in Palm Beach, Florida. A very successful musical play based on his life, *Billy Bishop Goes to War* by John Gray and starring Eric Peterson, was a huge financial and critical success across Canada in the late 1970s. It toured Canada, Great Britain and had a short run in New York. In the late 1990s the two artists staged a popular revival. Billy Bishop still projects a powerful image, over 75 years after his exploits.

Frank C. Williams Collection
NAC PA 122515 (detail)

Billy Bishop, the most decorated pilot of the First World War, in 1917.

BISHOP STREET

Bay/Davenport   There is some disagreement as to whether this street was named after the first Anglican bishop of Toronto, John Strachan (1778–1867), or John Bishop (1770–1845), a butcher. Born in London, England, John Bishop came to York via New York City with his wife and five children. Here, he opened one of York's first butcher shops, on the west side of Market Square. He lived with his family on Yonge St., north of Yorkville. He built a row of rental houses in 1833 at Adelaide and Simcoe streets, called Bishop's Block. Two of the houses are still standing in a parking lot at that corner (192 and 194 Adelaide St. West). See **STRACHAN AVE.**

Bishop's Block, circa 1885, on the northeast corner of Adelaide St. W. and Simcoe.

BLOOR STREET

TRL T 13662

Joseph Bloore, a brewer and faithful Methodist, developed land in the Yorkville area.

Broadview to Dixie between Queen/Queensway and Eglinton   This street was named after Joseph Bloore (1789–1862), who came to Canada from England in 1818 or 1819. He established the Farmers Arms Inn, just north of the St. Lawrence Market. In about 1830 he sold the inn and bought some land north of the Second Concession Line (now Bloor St.) near today's Sherbourne St. He built a brewery there and was very successful. He built himself a large house south of the concession road and east of Yonge. As the village of Yorkville grew, Bloore, along with his friend William Jarvis, got involved in land development in the area. The road leading from his brewery to Yorkville was first called Tollgate Rd., then St. Paul's Rd. (after St. Paul's Anglican Church, built in 1842), and, for a time, Sydenham St. By 1855 the name was changed to Bloor Street, and so it has remained ever since. Somewhere along the line, it lost the "e." A loyal Conservative and a faithful Methodist, when Bloore died a plaque was inscribed commemorating his life. It can still be seen in St. Andrew's United Church on Bloor St. East.

Two horses pull a steam-pumper past the Church of the Redeemer at Bloor and Avenue Rd. in 1912.

BLUE JAYS WAY

Front/Spadina   This was once the continuation of Peter St., named after Peter Russell (1731–1808), the first Administrator of the town of York. In 1993 the stretch of Peter St. running south from King St. was renamed Blue Jays Way, in honour of Toronto's major league baseball team, which had just won their second World Series championship in a row. The Blue Jays play their home games at SkyDome, situated at the foot of Peter. The name change was requested by Wayne Gretzky's Restaurant, which is located on that same street. The restaurant agreed to install a plaque commemorating Peter Russell (unveiled in November 1998). A second historical plaque commemorates Maple Leaf Stadium, which was home to Toronto's first professional baseball team, the Toronto Maple Leafs, until 1967. See **BASEBALL PLACE, PETER ST., STADIUM RD.**

BOND STREET

Queen/Yonge   There is some disagreement as to whether this street was named after Sir Francis Bond Head (1793–1875), the Lieutenant Governor of Upper Canada from 1835 until 1838; Thomas Bond, a brickmaker in the area in the 1840s; or John Bond, who had a cabinet shop on King St. East in the 1830s. Sir Francis Bond Head contributed to the Rebellion of 1837 by his hard-headed attitude to the Reformers. He was known by two colourful nicknames that suggest his somewhat rash and intractable character: Galloping Head (received when he was a mining supervisor in South America and given to wild rides across the rough terrain), and Bone Head, which speaks for itself. When he arrived in Upper Canada in 1836, he antagonized the Reformers,

TRL S 1-1138 J.V. Salmon (detail)

William Lyon Mackenzie lived for a time in this house on Bond St.

when, after appointing them to the Executive Council he proceeded to ignore their advice. They resigned. He called an election and won. His reactionary policies and alignment with the Family Compact inflamed the Reformers and led to the Rebellion in 1837. He dealt harshly with the rebels and was recalled by London early in 1838. He returned to England to write melodramatic memoirs. It is ironic that William Lyon Mackenzie, the leader of the Rebellion who was detested by Bond, lived for a time at 82 Bond St. The house has been restored and is now a museum. See **ROBERT ST.**

BONNYCASTLE STREET

Queen's Quay/Sherbourne   Sir Richard Henry Bonnycastle (1791–1847) of the Royal Engineers came to Upper Canada in 1826, after serving with his regiment in various campaigns. He prepared a report in 1834 for the local government in which he recommended the construction of a canal to open up the harbour from the east, and the drainage of the marsh at Ashbridge's Bay. However, his suggestions were not acted upon. In 1835 he asked Lieutenant Governor Sir John Colborne to make a request for an astronomical observatory to be built in Toronto by the British government. This was accomplished in 1840. He supervised the completion of two bridges in 1835 over the Don River, and then made a formal gift of them from the military to the city of Toronto. He also had a role to play in the Rebellion, while he was stationed at Kingston, building the new Fort Henry. After news of the attempted Rebellion in Toronto reached him, he gathered together workers, militia, Mohawks, sailors and other military personnel to form a garrison to protect Kingston. A group of rebels and American Sympathizers were planning to cross the St. Lawrence in February, 1838, but discouraged by the defences Bonnycastle had established at the fort, they withdrew.

BOULTON AVENUE
BOULTON DRIVE

Broadview/Gerrard; Davenport/Dupont   Boulton Ave. was named after James Boulton, a barrister. The Boulton family, prominent in the affairs of the city throughout the 19th century, had the dubious privilege of being named first when William Lyon Mackenzie listed the members of the Family Compact.

This elite group of Conservative Anglican families ran Upper Canada. D'Arcy Boulton Sr. (1759-1834) arrived in Upper Canada in about 1802. He became Solicitor General and Attorney General of the province, three of his sons were influential lawyers, and his grandson, William Henry Boulton (1812– 74), was mayor of Toronto. D'Arcy Boulton Jr. (1785–1846) built the Grange, a handsome dwelling that has been restored and is now part of the Art Gallery of Ontario. D'Arcy St., just north of the Grange, was laid out in the 1850s and named after D'Arcy Boulton Jr. See **GRANGE AVE.**

BRACONDALE HILL ROAD

Davenport/Ossington   Robert John Turner (1795–1872), a solicitor originally from Yarmouth, England, built an estate in 1842 called Bracondale north of present-day Davenport Rd. The house was located in what is now Hillcrest Park, at Christie and Davenport. Turner was the Accountant General of the Court of Chancery. The community that developed in and around the estate became known as Bracondale. It was annexed to the city of Toronto in 1909.

CTA SC 244 Item 42

The mud on Yonge St. near Balliol in 1913 paralyzed this car.

BRAEMORE GARDENS

Christie/Davenport
See **WYCHWOOD AVE.**

BRANT STREET

King/Spadina   Brant St. was named after Joseph Brant (1742–1807), whose Mohawk name was Thayendanega. He was a distinguished Mohawk chief who fought on the British side in the American Revolution and afterwards led his people to a new reserve on the banks of the Grand River in Upper Canada. He was a very cultivated, educated man who gained respect and admiration from the men he led in battle. He travelled to England twice to negotiate with the British government on behalf of his people. Brant worked for years to establish a confederation of Native peoples, but was ultimately unsuccessful. He established the Six Nations Reserve on the banks of the Grand River in 1785. A convert to Christianity, Brant worked to translate sections of the Bible into Mohawk. In 1785 he built the first Protestant church in Ontario, St. Paul's: Her Majesty's Chapel of the Mohawks, which still stands on the site of the original village. Joseph Brant is buried in a tomb outside the chapel. The city of Brantford was named after the place where Joseph Brant first forded the Oxford River when he settled with his people on the Six Nations Reserve.

THE BRIDLE PATH

Bayview/Lawrence   This street and area were named after the horseback riding trails that wound through the neighbourhood for the convenience of residents and riding club members. Edward Plunkett Taylor (1901–89), the businessman and racehorse owner, built his estate Windfields here. The area was first developed by Hubert Page, who bought a 50-acre farm on Bayview Ave. in 1929. His plan was to subdivide the land into smaller parcels and then sell them. The Depression crushed those plans, but he was still able to build a house for his family at the corner of the Bridle Path and Bayview Ave. E.P. Taylor built his house in 1936 and by 1947 there were half a dozen houses along the Bridle

Path. There are only two ways into the Bridle Path (the area was officially named in 1962): from Post Rd. and from Lawrence Ave. East near Edward's Gardens. It remains one of the most exclusive neighbourhoods in Toronto.

BROCK AVENUE

Dufferin/Queen   One might assume that this street was named after Sir Isaac Brock (1769–1812), the hero of the war of 1812, who died leading his troops at the Battle of Queenston Heights. But it was actually named after his cousin, James Brock (d. 1833), who owned land in the area. His widow, Lucy Brock, subdivided the land in 1850, with a road allowance from Lake Shore Blvd. to Bloor St. This road became known as Brockton Rd, and was changed later to Brock Ave. The village of Brockton, just west of Dufferin and Dundas, grew up in the area.

BROOKFIELD STREET

Ossington/Queen   Brookfield House was the name John Denison (1757–1824) gave to the house he built at the corner of what is today the northwest corner of Queen and Ossington. The Denisons were an influential family in Toronto for over 100 years. The house passed to John's wife, Sophia, at his death, who gave it to her son-in-law, John Fennings Taylor, in 1845. The Lunatic Asylum was built across the street in 1846, and the house eventually was demolished and the land sold. Brookfield St. was named after the house, Ossington Ave. after Ossington House, the family seat in Nottinghamshire in England, and Rolyat St. was named after John Taylor (Taylor spelt backwards). See **BELLE-VUE AVE., DENISON AVE., DOVERCOURT RD., HEYDON PARK RD., RUSHOLME RD.**

BRUCE PARK AVENUE

Bayview/Eglinton   Herbert Alexander Bruce (1868–1963) was a surgeon, military officer, university professor and politician, who is perhaps best remembered as the founder of Wellesley Hospital in 1912. He served as Special Inspector General of the Canadian Army Medical Corps during the First World War. In 1920 Bruce purchased a farm on Bayview Ave., the second lot south of Lawrence, overlooking the Don Valley. The property had been farmed by the Jones family for 90 years, and Bruce built a grand Tudor-style mansion on the foundation of the Jones farmhouse, using Eden Smith as the architect. Dr. Bruce named his house Annandale, after the Scottish hero and king, Robert Bruce (1274–1329), Lord of Annandale and King of Scotland. He sold it in 1929 and built another house, which he christened with the same name, at Steeles and Bayview. He was Lieutenant Governor of Ontario from 1932 to 1937, elected to Parliament in 1940 and 1945, and served on the Board of Directors of the University of Toronto. See **ANNAN DR., WYCHWOOD AVE.**

BRULÉ CRESCENT
BRULÉ GARDENS
BRULÉ TERRACE

Bloor/Kingsway   Étienne Brulé (1592–1632) was a French explorer and interpreter who was the first European to see four of the five Great Lakes. He lived with the Hurons for nearly 20 years, learning their languages and making many explorations throughout eastern Canada and the United States, which unfortunately he did not document. During his campaign against the Iroquois in 1615, Samuel de Champlain (1570–1635) sent Brulé ahead through enemy territory with 12 Huron braves. Brulé followed the Humber River to its mouth on Lake Ontario and became the first white man to see the future site of the city of Toronto, in September 1615. He was captured and tortured by the Iroquois on the way back, but he eventually escaped. Brulé adopted Native customs and living habits and was disapproved of by his fellow Europeans. In 1629 he sided with the English against Champlain and was accused of treason by the French. He went back to live among the Hurons. In 1633, probably as the result of a quarrel, the Hurons killed him and ate him.

Étienne Brulé at the mouth of the Humber, 1615. Charles William Jeffreys.

BRUNSWICK AVENUE

Bathurst/College   Brunswick is a city and region in Germany and the name of a royal line, the House of Brunswick. This street was probably named after either the House of Brunswick or Caroline Brunswick of Wolfenbüttel

(1768–1821), the wife of King George IV of England (b. 1762, r. 1820–30). She was the second daughter of Charles William, Duke of Brunswick-Wolfenbüttel, and King George's first cousin. He didn't like her much and made her live apart from him. He tried to divorce her but she had considerable public sympathy and the Divorce Bill he brought to Parliament was defeated. See **GEORGE ST.**

BUCKINGHAM AVENUE

Lawrence/Mount Pleasant   Buckingham is a town in England, situated in Buckinghamshire. The Earldom of Buckingham dates back to the 12th century. In the early 1700s, John Sheffield, the Duke of Buckingham, built a mansion he named Buckingham House. In 1761 King George III (b. 1738, r. 1760–1820) bought Buckingham House for his wife, Queen Charlotte, and it was renamed the Queen's House. His son, George IV (b. 1762, r. 1820–30) began work in 1826 to change it into a palace, under the supervision of the architect John Nash. George IV never lived there, but in 1837 Queen Victoria moved in three weeks after her accession to the throne, and Buckingham Palace became the official royal residence in London, undergoing many renovations and additions over the years.

BULWER STREET

Queen/Spadina   Edward Bulwer-Lytton (1803–73) was a popular English novelist, poet, playwright and politician who became the first Baron Lytton. He is best remembered for his historical novel, *The Last Days of Pompeii* (1834). He was a Member of Parliament and in 1858–59 served as Secretary for the Colonies. This street was named in 1876, just three years after his death.

BYNG AVENUE

Finch/Yonge   Julian Hedworth George Byng (1862–1935), known as Viscount Byng of Vimy, served as Governor General of Canada from 1921 to 1926. In May 1916 Byng was appointed the commander of the Canadian Corps. Less than a year later, his troops defeated the enemy at Vimy Ridge in one of the bloodiest battles of the Great War. He was named Baron Byng of Vimy, and came to Canada as Governor General in 1921. In Canada, Byng is chiefly remembered for his part in the King-Byng Affair in 1925, when the minority Mackenzie King Liberal government appealed to him to dissolve Parliament and he refused. The Conservatives, led by Arthur Meighen, formed a government but then were defeated on a vote. Byng dissolved Parliament and an election was called. According to parliamentary rules of procedure he behaved correctly, but Canadians resented it anyway. Byng returned to England the next year.

CAMBRAI AVENUE

Danforth/Main   Cambrai is a town in northern France that was liberated in the First World War by Canadian troops on October 9, 1918. The original Cambrai Ave. was never built. At the turn of the century Toronto city planners began to be influenced by the City Beautiful Movement, which was influential in city design in Europe and the United States. The movement called for large public squares with wide streets radiating out from them, and monuments, galleries, parks and improved transportation. In 1909 a City Improvement Committee was formed and many changes to the city were proposed. Building the Bloor St. Viaduct was one improvement that was realized, but another plan never got off the drawing board: Federal Ave. It was to run from Front St. up to Queen, and end in a grand public square with large government buildings beside Osgoode Hall, in about the spot where the New City Hall and Nathan Phillips Square stand today. A modified version of the project was revived in 1929, with Federal Ave. renamed Cambrai Ave., with a public memorial to the Canadians who fought there. But as Canada hovered on the brink of the Depression, this plan too fell through. Eventually additions to the Royal York Hotel filled up the space that might have become the grandest avenue in Toronto.

· CAMBRAI AVENUE · LOOKING NORTH FROM KING ST ·

A 1929 drawing of the proposed Cambrai Ave., looking north from King St.

CAMPBELL CRESCENT

Yonge/York Mills   Chief Justice Sir William Campbell (1758–1834) was born in Scotland. He fought in a Highland Regiment in 1775 in the American Revolutionary War and was taken prisoner. In 1785 he settled in Nova Scotia, where he studied law. By 1811, he was a judge in Upper Canada, and in 1825 he succeeded Chief Justice Powell. Four years later Campbell became the first Canadian judge to be knighted. Campbell was instrumental in building

Osgoode Hall in 1822, and he served for a time as the Speaker of the Legislative Assembly. Today he is remembered by pedestrians who pass his house at the northwest corner of Queen St. West and University, opposite Osgoode Hall. Campbell House and the Grange, which are both Georgian structures, are the two oldest brick houses remaining in Toronto. Sir William built his house in 1822 at the corner of Duke St. (Adelaide) and Frederick, where he had a lovely view of the bay. After his death his wife lived there until 1844. Then the house went through many transformations, somehow retaining its basic structure while it was used for a vinegar warehouse, a glass warehouse, an elevator company and a factory for making horseshoe nails. It was nearly demolished to make a parking lot in 1971, but the Advocates' Society, a group of trial lawyers, raised the money to move all 300 tons of it to its present location. The house was lovingly restored and can now be toured as a museum.

In 1972 Campbell House moves slowly (600 feet per hour) to its new location at Queen and University. Reprinted with permission from *The Globe and Mail* March 31, 1972.

CARLING AVENUE

Bloor/Ossington This street is named after the Honourable John Carling (1828–1911), who was the heir to Carling Breweries in London, Ontario, established in 1843 by his father, Thomas C. Carling. In 1857 John Carling won a seat for the Conservatives and served in both the Provincial and the Federal Parliaments. He was Postmaster General from 1882 to 1885, Minister of Agriculture from 1867 to 1871, and sat in the Senate from 1891 to 1892 and from 1896 to 1911. In 1893 he was knighted.

CARLTON STREET

Gerrard/Parliament Ann Wood, daughter of Dr. George Wood, married Andrew McGill, who had made a fortune in the fur trade. After he died, she married John Strachan. They owned 25 acres north of Gerrard St., parts of which they donated to the city in 1834. Ann named Carlton St. after her brother, Guy Carleton Wood, who was named after Guy Carleton (1724–1808), Lord Dorchester. He fought against the French in Quebec in 1759, and served as the Lieutenant Governor of Quebec from 1766 to 1768, and as Governor from 1768 to 1778 and from 1785 to 1795. Somewhere along the way, the "e" dropped out of Carleton. McGill St. was named after Ann. Carlton St. originally met Yonge St. south of College, but it was eventually joined to College by means of a sharp jog just west of Church St. See **SIMCOE ST., STRACHAN AVE., UNIVERSITY AVE.**

CASIMIR STREET

Bathurst/Dundas Sir Casimir Stanislaus Gzowski (1813–98) was born in St. Petersburg, Russia, the son of a Polish count. He trained as an engineer and served in the Polish army. In 1833 he was exiled because of his involvement in the Polish revolt, and he sailed to the United States, where to get by he taught the violin, fencing and languages. He studied to be a lawyer, worked as an engineer on the New York and Erie Railway and eventually moved to Canada, where Lord Sydenham, the Governor General, helped him obtain a job with

NAC C 008620 NLC

A Polish exile and engineer, Sir Casimir Gzowski was a leading figure in Toronto business and society.

the Canadian Public Works Department. Among his many impressive projects were the International Bridge at Niagara Falls, the Erie Canal, the Grand Trunk Railway and the park system on the Canadian side of Niagara Falls. Gzowski bought a piece of property on Bathurst St. between Queen and Dundas. His Victorian home, christened the "Hall," stood in lavish grounds with a deer park, bowling green and exotic birds. He entertained expansively and gained a reputation as one of the more romantic figures in Toronto's history. In 1890 he was knighted. Gzowski was one of the founders of the Toronto Stock Exchange and served as president of the Toronto Turf Club, the Toronto Philharmonic Society, and the London and Canada Loan Company. His house was demolished in 1904 and part of his estate was made into Alexandrea Park. One of his descendants is the popular radio personality and author, Peter Gzowski. See **SYDENHAM ST.**

CASTLE FRANK CRESCENT
CASTLE FRANK ROAD

TRL T 16776

The intrepid Elizabeth Simcoe slept in a tent and picnicked on the banks of the Don River.

Bloor/Parliament When John Graves Simcoe (1752–1806), the first Lieutenant Governor of Upper Canada, came to lay out the town of York as the capital of the new province in 1792, he brought with him his adventurous wife, Elizabeth (1762–1850), and two of their small children, Sophia and Francis. They lived in large tents in town and went on expeditions up the picturesque Don River. Elizabeth decided to build a summer cottage on a hill overlooking the river, and she whimsically named it Castle Frank, registering the land in the little boy's name. It was a very simple structure made from logs, with upright logs as columns at one end. They never lived there, but would stay overnight sometimes and have parties and picnics on the site. The Simcoes returned to England in 1796 and the house eventually fell into disrepair and was accidentally burned down by fishermen. Little Francis grew up to join the army and was killed in action at the age of 20 in the Spanish Peninsular War. Many years later Edward Kemp built a much grander Castle Frank slightly north of the original. Rosedale Heights Secondary School now occupies that site. See **SIMCOE ST.**

Elizabeth Simcoe sketched her beloved Castle Frank in 1796 from just east of the Don River.

CASTLEFIELD AVENUE
CASTLEWOOD ROAD
CASTLE KNOCK ROAD

Yonge/Eglinton; Avenue Rd./Eglinton In 1832 a man named James Hervey Price (1797–1882) bought 200 acres of land just north of Eglinton, between Bathurst and Yonge. He built a miniature castle that resembled the house where he grew up in Chelsea, England. He named his new house Castlefield after his English home. With its Gothic windows, four turrets and large central hall, it is no surprise that locals began referring to it as the Castle. The driveway to his house became Castlefield Ave. Today Castlefield Ave. is interrupted for a few blocks by Allen Rd., but it does continue west almost as far as Keele St. Price, a lawyer who was the first City Clerk for the town of York, supported William Lyon Mackenzie and the Reformers, but he didn't take an active part in the Rebellion. Some stories report that Mackenzie hid in the Castle in a baby's cradle and was saved by the cook, who scolded the officers

TRL T 15010 JRR

James Hervey Price built his house with four turrets to look like a miniature castle.

who came looking for him, telling them not to wake the baby. Price was jailed for 13 days because of his association with Mackenzie. His land was sold in 1842 to Franklin Jackes, who was the first Reeve of York Township. Jackes uncovered the remains of an Indian village on the property and the artefacts ended up in the Royal Ontario Museum. Castlefield was demolished in 1920. See **WILLOWBANK BLVD.**

CAWTHRA SQUARE

Jarvis/Wellesley   William Cawthra (1801–80) was a very rich financier and politician with business connections in New York and Britain. In 1854 he built a grand house, designed by Joseph Sheard, at King and Bay. After his death his widow moved to another mansion at Isabella and Jarvis, very near the spot where Cawthra Square stands today.

CHAPLIN CRESCENT

Avenue Rd./Eglinton   There are two versions of the source of this name, and they may both be part of the same story. One is that a family called Chaplin from St. Catharines bought this land. Another says that a man named William Chaplin from North Toronto lived in the area and the street was named after him. What is clear is that this land was originally part of the Clergy Reserves, which were large parcels of land set aside for the Protestant Church, which in those days in Upper Canada meant the Anglican Church. The Clergy Reserves were the source of great controversy in the 19th century. They comprised a huge amount of land: one-seventh of all public lands. They were meant to be used for building churches and rectories, and they could be sold to finance the Church. The other Protestant denominations, the Presbyterians, Methodists and the Church of Scotland, wanted some share of these lands. It became one of the burning issues of the Rebellion in 1837. In 1840 the new Governor General, Lord Sydenham, helped to get an act through the Legislative Assembly that provided for the sale of Clergy Reserves and the division of the profits among the various denominations. The Chaplin Estates was a seven-block area that was subdivided in 1913. Houses were built in 1923. See **COLBORNE ST., STRACHAN AVE., SYDENHAM ST.**

CHESTNUT PARK ROAD

Summerhill/Yonge   Senator David Macpherson (1818–96) was a financier and politician who built the Grand Trunk Railway with Casimir Gzowski. Knighted in 1884, Macpherson was a member of the Senate and served as Minister of the Interior for the Conservative government of Sir John A. Macdonald. He retired from politics in 1885 after criticism of the way he had handled the Northwest Rebellion. Macpherson married Elizabeth Molson, of the Molson brewing family, in 1844 and in 1855 bought a piece of property and a house on the east side of Yonge St., north of Bloor. With the help of an architect he made many improvements and additions to the house. He named it Chestnut Park after the grand avenue of chestnut trees that led up the driveway to the mansion. The home was famous for its conservatories. St. Andrew's College, now in Aurora, used the house between 1899 and 1904, when the house was demolished. See **CASIMIR ST.**

CHICORA AVENUE

Avenue Rd./Dupont   This street was probably named after the steamship Chicora, which was built in Liverpool in 1864 and rebuilt in Toronto in 1878. The ship sailed the Great Lakes and the St. Lawrence River between 1878 and 1919, when it sank in the Toronto harbour. It was hauled up, converted into a barge in 1920 and used until 1939 when it sank again, this time off Howe Island, near Kingston, Ontario. The ship's remains can still be spotted underwater in the Bateau Channel. The Chicora was the first ship of the Niagara Navigation Company, which eventually owned five ships, all beginning with the letter "C": Chicora, Cibola, Chippewa, Corona and Cayuga.

CHRISTIE STREET

Bathurst/Bloor   William Mellis Christie (1829–99) came to Canada in 1848 from Scotland, where he had been an apprentice to a biscuit maker. In 1849 he went to work in the bakery of Mathers and Brown. He eventually went into partnership with Brown and the firm flourished. They built a huge factory at

Duke (Adelaide) and Frederick streets, and shipped cookies across the country. After Brown retired, Christie took over and the company kept thriving. When Christie died in 1899, his son Robert Jaffray Christie took over as president. Their company continued to be successful throughout the 20th century and into the 21st. It is now owned by Nabisco Ltd., but still sells cookies under the name Christie.

CHURCH STREET

Esplanade to Bloor between Jarvis and Yonge   Church St. was named after the first church in the town of York, which stood on the site of St. James' Cathedral at the corner of King and Church. The Cathedral is the fourth church to occupy this spot. The first church, completed in 1807, was a very simple wooden building surrounded by forest, which was simply referred to as the Church at York. The church formed the centre of the social scene in early York. As was the custom then, families paid for their pews and whoever paid the most got the best seats. In 1812 John Strachan (1778–1867) was appointed the rector,

Looking north on Church St. from Front circa 1890.

CTA SC 478 Item 36

and when the invading Yankee army looted it in April 1813, Strachan stopped them from destroying the church and the rest of York by demanding terms of surrender. In 1828 the Church was dedicated as St. James and in 1832 a second church was built of stone. Strachan was appointed the first bishop of Toronto in 1839 and St. James became a Cathedral just before it was destroyed by fire. The Cathedral was rebuilt (church number three), but it burned down in the Great Fire of 1849 that destroyed most of the downtown area. Strachan planned a grand new cathedral in the Gothic Revival style, which was popular in England at the time. It opened for worship in 1853 but the tower and spire were not completed until 1856 and 1874. A marble baptismal font in the West Porch remains the only survivor from the previous church. Once one of the tallest structures in the city, it is now dwarfed by Toronto's many skyscrapers. However, you can still catch glimpses of the steeple from various parts of the downtown area, and easily imagine how it was once a focal point of the city's skyline. See **STRACHAN AVE., TRINITY CIRCLE.**

[AO F 4357-0-0-10 S15334 check credit number]

Carriages lined up outside St. James' Cathedral on a cold winter day in 1870.

CLARENCE SQUARE

King/Spadina   In 1834 there was a plan to build a new Government House in the area bounded by King, Peter, Front and Spadina. The site was named Clarence Square, in honour of Prince William Henry (1765–1837), Duke of Clarence, the third son of George III, who was to become William IV of England in 1830. Although Government House never was built here (they chose a site a couple of blocks to the east instead), eventually several fashionable homes were built on the square. William IV, known as "Silly Billy," was an eccentric king who liked to spit in public and pick up strangers to give them lifts in his carriage. He won public approval by slashing costs at his coronation. King William was determined to stay alive until his niece (the future Queen Victoria) was old enough to rule, in order to thwart her mother, the Duchess of Kent, whom he swore he would never allow to be Regent. He managed to survive until one month after Victoria reached her majority at the age of 18. See **PARLIAMENT ST., QUEEN ST.**

CLARENDON AVENUE

Avenue Rd./St. Clair   This street was probably named for George William Frederick Villiers (1800–70), the 4th Earl of Clarendon, a diplomat and politician who was Britain's Secretary of State for Foreign Affairs from 1853 to 1855 and again in 1865 and 1868. In this position he took on the responsibility for the Crimean War.

COLBORNE STREET

King/Yonge   Sir John Colborne (1778–1863) was the Lieutenant Governor of Upper Canada from 1828 to 1836. A distinguished military officer, he commanded the 52nd Light Infantry at the Battle of Waterloo in 1815, leading them in from the right in a famous manoeuvre that finally defeated the French Guard. He was known to his soldiers as "auld grog Willie" because of the extra rum he gave them. Colborne came to Canada in 1828 after seven years as the Lieutenant Governor of Guernsey. He came to a colony ripe with unrest, with the Family Compact, Bishop John Strachan and the conservative establishment lined up against various degrees of Reformers led by William Lyon Mackenzie. Colborne used his experience to try to steer a moderate, conservative course, and was successful on many fronts: he encouraged British immigration; improved communications, transportation and markets; and personally paid for the repair of the bridges over the Don and Humber Rivers. Where he faltered was in the area of religion and schools, where his actions favoured the Anglican elite and enraged the Reformers. Colborne founded Upper Canada College in 1829, a private boys school geared to teach the sons of the Anglican ruling class. To set up the school, he arranged to divert funds that were reserved for public schools and universities. In 1836 he allocated the Clergy Reserves and some Crown land for the endowment of Anglican rectories. This issue, which had been developing over a number of years, was one of the direct causes of the Rebellion of 1837. In 1836 Colborne was replaced as Lieutenant Governor and placed in charge of British troops in the Canadas. In that role he put down the Rebellion in Lower Canada in 1837 and earned a new nickname, perhaps unfairly, as "le Vieux Brulôt," due to the brutality of his men during that campaign. Colborne left Canada for England in 1839, where he was named a privy councillor and raised to a peer as Lord Seaton. Another place in Toronto

Architect John Howard named Colborne Lodge in honour of his patron, Sir John Colborne. Circa 1920.

still holds his name: Colborne Lodge, in High Park, which was the home of his protegé, John George Howard (1803–90), the architect and city surveyor who began his career teaching drawing at Upper Canada College. See **CHAPLIN CRESCENT, HOWARD PARK AVE., STRACHAN AVE.**

COLGATE AVENUE

Queen/Pape   Formerly Natalie St., this name was changed to Colgate at the request of the Colgate-Palmolive Peet Company, whose factory was located there. It has since been torn down. William Colgate, who lived from 1783 to 1857, was an American manufacturer. Born in England, he arrived in the United States in 1795 and in 1806 set up a tallow factory in New York that

Workers at the Colgate factory in Toronto in January, 1919.

produced starch, soap and candles. The factory moved to Jersey City in 1847 and over the years the company expanded to produce perfumed soaps, perfumes and toothpaste. It joined with the Palmolive Peet Company in 1928. William Colgate organized Bible societies and donated some of his fortune to Colgate University.

COLLEGE STREET

Yonge to Lansdowne between Dundas and Bloor
See **UNIVERSITY AVE.**

CONACHER DRIVE

Bayview/Steeles   Charles William (Charlie) Conacher (1909–68) was one of 10 children who lived in a working-class district of Toronto on Davenport Rd. and attended Jesse Ketchum School. Charlie played with the National Hockey League between 1929 and 1941, mostly for the Toronto Maple Leafs. He scored the first Leafs' goal in the new Maple Leaf Gardens, which opened in November 1931. With Joe Primeau and Harvey Jackson, Conacher formed the "Kid Line" in 1929: their combined ages were 58. He won the scoring title (Art Ross Trophy) in 1934 and 1935. After his career as a hockey player ended, Charlie Conacher went on to coach the Chicago Black Hawks and was eventually elected to the Hockey Hall of Fame.

CONNABLE DRIVE

Bathurst/St. Clair   Ralph Connable, an American from Chicago, took over as Canadian manager of the F.W. Woolworth Company in 1912. He moved his family to Toronto and built a house on Lyndhurst Ave., which was admired as one of the grand houses of the area, with stunning gardens designed by the founders of Sheridan Nurseries. While under Connable's management, the Canadian Woolworth's grew from an initial 10 stores to 100, making it the biggest chain store in Canada. During the First World War, the Canadian government drew on Connable's expertise to improve its spending habits, and he successfully eliminated millions of dollars of waste. Ernest Hemingway, an acquaintance from Chicago, lived with the Connables for a time and tutored their disabled son. After he retired, Connable moved back to the United States. His handsome mansion eventually became a rehabilitation hospital, Lyndhurst Lodge.

CONSTANCE STREET

Dundas/Roncesvalles
See **O'HARA AVE.**

COPELAND STREET

Eglinton/Laird   In the 19th century, Copland was a name associated with beer. The spelling of this street was changed somewhere along the line. Copland's Brewery was built in 1832 on the lower section of Yonge St. in the heart of Muddy York's downtown area. Its owner and creator, William Copland, opened smaller breweries, one on Queen St. East and another at the corner of Yonge and Bloor. In 1847 he built the East Toronto Brewery at the corner of King St. East and Parliament. By the early 1880s this brewery was the largest in Toronto, with five acres of cellars, vaults and ice houses that could store 4,000 tons of ice. It turned out 25,000 barrels of beer, ale and stout annually. Copland's son sold the enterprise and in 1946 Labatt's Brewery took over and the plant was closed.

COTTINGHAM ROAD
COTTINGHAM STREET

Spadina/Davenport   Like so many streets in Toronto, Cottingham Rd. was named after the British birthplace of one of the early citizens of the area,

Peter Hutty (1819–82), who was born in Cottingham, Yorkshire. Hutty was a butcher and a member of the first council of the village of Yorkville (amalgamated into Toronto in 1883). He lived at the corner of Yonge St. and Cottingham, and supplied beef to the provincial government and the military garrisoned in the city. He also had a stall at the St. Lawrence Market. He served as a member of the Yorkville Village Council for more than 13 years. He was reeve for a couple of years, when he supported the construction of the Town Hall and Jesse Ketchum School. As one of the original members of the Yorkville Village Council, he is represented in the Yorkville coat of arms by the bull in the centre and the letter "H." You can still see the coat of arms above the door on the firehall on Yorkville Ave. There was also a Cottingham School, which stood from 1877 till 1955 on Cottingham near Birch Ave. See **CUMBERLAND ST., SEVERN ST.**

COXWELL AVENUE

Lake Shore Blvd. to O'Connor between Woodbine and Greenwood   Charles Coxwell Small (1800–64) was the youngest son of Major John Small (1746–1831), who was the Clerk of the Executive Council of Upper Canada and lived in a house called Berkeley on King St. East. Charles became a clerk of the Crown in Pleas of the King's Bench Division of the Supreme Court in 1825. The Berkeley estate included a large tract of land bounded by Danforth, Coxwell, Woodbine and Lake Ontario. Charles developed his property by building sawmills and a tannery, and he raised prize-winning cattle on his farm. See **BERKELEY ST.**

CROFT STREET

Bathurst/College   This street commemorates the life of John Croft (1866–1904), a part-time dynamiter who was killed in an accident after the great fire of April 19–20, 1904. The worst fire in the history of Toronto broke out downtown, at 58 Wellington St., just west of Bay. By the time it was finally extinguished by the combined efforts of 250 firemen nine hours later, the fire had destroyed 123 buildings, obliterated 139 businesses, and put 5,000 people out of work. Croft volunteered to help blow up the ruins of a building on Front St. On May 4, after only two charges out of three detonated, he waited for a few minutes and then attempted to defuse it. The dynamite exploded in his face and he died the next morning of his injuries.

Bay St. lies in ruins after the great fire in 1904.

CUMBERLAND STREET

Avenue Rd./Bloor   Like Cottingham St., Cumberland St. was named after the birthplace of one of the first councillors of the village of Yorkville, James Wallis (b. 1807). The former county of Cumberland (now joined with

Westmorland County to form Cumbria) lies in the north of England on the boundary of Scotland, in the Lake District. During the Roman occupation of Britain, the Roman Emperor Hadrian (76–138) built his famous Hadrian's Wall here, between 122 and 126 C.E. The Border Wars between England and Scotland were fought in and around Cumberland over the course of 500 years, from about 1300 to 1800. James Wallis, a blacksmith, was represented on the Yorkville coat of arms by the letter "W" and an anvil. After he left the council he served as treasurer for several years. See **COTTINGHAM ST., HADRIAN DR., SEVERN ST., WESTMORELAND AVE.**

CUMMER AVENUE

Bayview/Finch   This street was named after the Kummer family (sometimes spelt Cummer), early settlers in the area. They were Lutherans who were forced to leave Germany because of their religion, and then, because they were loyal to Britain, they left Pennsylvania after the American Revolution to live in Canada. Jacob Kummer (1767–1841), who came to Canada in 1797, bought land east of Yonge St. between Sheppard and Finch. He gradually bought up more land near Finch and Bayview and built a sawmill there in 1819. For many years, the street named after the Kummers was little more than a track cleared for horses and buggies that extended east from Yonge to the Don River, where the Kummer sawmill stood. Over the next 50 years the Kummers built more mills and a woollen factory and operated the Willowdale post office (established in 1855) in a shop on Yonge above Finch, where they sold stovepipes and pots and pans. The Kummers converted to Methodism and held rousing camp meetings at their mill. The area subsequently was called Scripture Town and then Angel Valley. A story survives from this family's early years. Jacob's wife, Elizabeth, alone with her children, was unexpectedly visited by a Native who seemed transfixed by a large knife lying on the kitchen table. Afraid, she gave it to him. A few days later he returned with a cradle he had built for her baby, fulfilling his people's custom of giving a gift in return for a gift, and thus extending welcome to the new Canadians.

DALTON ROAD

Bloor/Spadina   This street was named after the Dalton family, probably either Thomas Dalton (1782–1840) or his son Robert Gladstone Dalton (1819–92). Originally from Birmingham, England, Thomas came first to St. John's, Newfoundland, in 1810 and then to Kingston in 1817, where he established a brewery. He got into banking, then politics and finally journalism, leaving a trail of debts, disasters and failed enterprises behind him. In 1829 he started a newspaper, the *Patriot and Farmer's Monitor*. He expressed fairly radical views and in 1832 moved to York. Once in the capital, he underwent something of a sea change, antagonized his former associates, especially William Lyon Mackenzie, and took a more traditional stance. Dalton was known for extremely strong language in his writing, which his wife, Sophia Simms Dalton, had to edit to avoid libel. When he died in 1840 she took over running the biweekly paper. Toronto's first woman publisher, she managed the paper for eight years and then sold it in 1848.

DANFORTH AVENUE
DANFORTH ROAD

Kingston Rd. to Broadview between Gerrard and O'Connor/St. Clair; Danforth and Warden to Lawrence and McCowan   Asa Danforth (1746–1836) was an American contractor who was commissioned to build a road between York and Kingston. This he did, using a route along today's Queen St. East to Kingston Road and Danforth Rd., completing it in 1800. Danforth was constantly plagued by debt, and the government at York didn't help. Their payments were supposed to be made as he completed each section of the road, but they were always slow and in 1800 refused to pay him the balance owing until the road was properly finished. He left Canada in disgust and for a while tried do foment rebellion by meeting with groups of like-minded Canadians in Albany, New York. However, it all came to naught and Danforth spent the rest of his life struggling against his debts. He never had anything to do with building Danforth Ave., which in the 1880s served to connect Broadview to Danforth Rd., which was the main eastern highway. Many mills and connected industries thrived in the Don Valley, and small communities grew up near them: Todmorden, Doncaster and Chester. These areas were annexed to Toronto in 1909. Until 1919, when the Prince Edward Viaduct was built to link the Danforth to downtown, the main route across the Don River was the bridge at the foot of Winchester St., which then turned north to join up with the Danforth, going up the hill about where the on-ramp to the Don Valley north is. After the Viaduct was built the Danforth developed quickly, as commercial buildings were constructed along its length and residential areas grew up nearby. See **TODMORDEN LANE.**

CTA RG8 10 Item 841

Constructing the Prince Edward Viaduct, July 18, 1917.

Winchester St. used to curve northeast across the Don River to meet the Danforth at Broadview. Circa 1870.

D'ARCY STREET

Dundas/Spadina

See **BOULTON AVE.**

D'ARCY MAGEE CRESCENT

Lawrence/Port Union   Thomas D'Arcy McGee (1825–68) was known as one of the most eloquent Fathers of Confederation. Born in Ireland, he immigrated to the United States and worked on a newspaper in Boston for a few years, then went back to Ireland. He was involved in the Rebellion of 1848 and had to leave in a hurry. He worked as a journalist in the United States for 10 years, then came to Montreal in 1857 to work on the *New Era*, a new newspaper dedicated to a "new nationality." In 1858 he was elected as a member of the Legislative Assembly and soon joined John A. Macdonald and George-Étienne Cartier in their political aims. He was in attendance at the Charlottetown and Quebec conferences in September and October of 1864 that led to Confederation. Magee was a poet and a historian as well as a journalist, publishing more than 300 poems and several books on Irish history. His outspoken opposition to the Fenians and their plots to conquer Canada probably led to his assassination in 1868. His murderers were never found.

DARTNELL AVENUE

Bathurst/Davenport   Dartnell is named after Georgina Dartnell. Her father, George Russell Dartnell, was a painter and the surgeon for the regiment in which Frederick Wells (1822–77) served. While in Canada with the British army between 1835 and 1844, Dartnell produced more than 150 pictures. Frederick was the son of Colonel Joseph Wells (1773–1853), who owned the Davenport estate. Frederick had a successful army career and was awarded medals by both Napoleon III of France and the Sultan of Turkey for his role in the Crimean War. He inherited Davenport and married Georgina in 1866. She died giving birth to their second child, a daughter (Nina Frederica), in 1875, and Frederick took his children away from the scene of the tragedy, to England, where he died two years later. See **DAVENPORT RD., NINA ST., WELLS HILL AVE.**

DAVENPORT ROAD

Bloor/Yonge   Davenport Rd. was originally a Native portage trail from the Don to the Humber River. It probably ran along the same route as the Rosedale Valley Rd. The name Davenport was taken from the home of Colonel Joseph Wells (1773–1853), which stood approximately at the northeast corner of Bathurst and Davenport. Wells, a war hero who fought at Badajos in the Napoleonic Wars, came to Canada in 1815 and bought the house and property from Adjutant John McGill in 1821. McGill supposedly named his house after a certain Major Davenport, who was stationed at Fort York in 1797, when the house was built. Wells rebuilt the house, and his family and descendants lived there until it was torn down in 1913. The location provided a marvellous view of Lake Ontario. An active member of York society, Joseph Wells served on the Legislative Council and the Executive Council and as a director for the Bank of Upper Canada. His stint as the treasurer of Upper Canada College ended in disgrace when the books were found to be in a complete mess, with receipts and accounts floating in and out of his pockets. After Davenport was built, other fancy estates followed along the brow of the hill: Spadina, Russell Hill, Chestnut Park, Wychwood, Benvenuto, Glen Edyth and Casa Loma. Davenport Rd. became a toll road, much travelled by farmers bringing their produce to market. Dupont St., Wells St. and Wells Hill Ave. were named after Joseph Wells' eldest son, George Dupont Wells (1814–1854), who was one of the first students at Upper Canada College. See **DARTNELL AVE., NINA ST.**

Looking south to Davenport Rd. from the crest of the Lansdowne Ave. hill, 1931.

CTA/TTC Fonds Series 71 Item 8319

DAVIES AVENUE

Broadview/Queen   Formerly Mill St., this street was renamed Davies Ave. in 1884 after Thomas Davies (1813–69), a prominent brewer in the area. He emigrated from Cheshire, England, in 1832 and in 1849 established a brewery near the Don River, at Queen and River streets. He lived at 33 River St. with his wife Fidelia Jones and his seven children, and his brewery prospered and grew. By 1872 the Davies clan was selling 3,500 gallons per day. His motto was "A man never died of hard work." His son, Thomas Davies Jr., was in municipal politics for 40 years. An alderman in the city of Toronto, Thomas was instrumental in paving streets and sidewalks and naming High Park and Riverdale Park. Thomas was responsible for straightening the Don River below Gerrard St. after severe flooding in 1878.

DAVISVILLE AVENUE

St. Clair/Yonge   Davisville was an incorporated village clustered around the area of Yonge and Davisville until 1889, when it joined with the village of Eglinton to form the village of North Toronto, which became part of Toronto in 1912. Davisville drew its name from John Davis, who came to Canada from England in 1840 and learned the pottery business. In 1845 he established his own pottery on Yonge St. at Davisville, using clay from deposits nearby. Davis Pottery became famous across the country, first for producing earthenware, flowerpots and cream jars, then by expanding into green-glazed rose jars and jardinieres and winning numerous prizes at provincial exhibitions. The pottery moved to 377 Merton and then to 601 Merton and was in business until 1932. John Davis was the first postmaster in the area; he helped to build Davisville School and he served as a school trustee for 25 years. In 1851 he founded the Davisville Methodist Church in a log cabin and in 1866 he donated land at Yonge and Belsize for a new Methodist church to be built. The church was demolished in the 1960s. After his death, John Davis' sons carried on his business and were active in the community.

DEER PARK CRESCENT

St. Clair/Yonge   Deer Park was a village at Yonge and St. Clair that drew its name from the herds of tame deer that roamed the area. Deer Park Crescent used to be the driveway up to the farm named Deer Park. Agnes Heath bought 40 acres just west of Yonge and north of St. Clair in 1837 and called her estate Deer Park. She was the widow of Colonel Charles Heath, who died in India in 1818. The deer were a notable feature of the area and wandered up to local hotels to be fed by the guests. Michael O'Halloran's Deer Park Hotel on the southwest corner of St. Clair and Yonge was one of their favourite feeding spots. Agnes' son, Charles Wallace Heath, was a soldier who fought with the Royal Dragoons in the Rebellion of 1837. He became a lawyer and was one of the original founders of the Toronto Boat Club in 1850, which by 1854 had evolved into the Royal Canadian Yacht Club. In 1846 Charles bought the farm from his mother and had it subdivided into 33 lots, which were mostly sold by 1850. Heath St. was named after the family.

DEGRASSI STREET

Broadview/Queen   This street was named after the De Grassi family, probably either Captain Phillipe De Grassi (1793–1874), who bought land to farm in the Don Valley in 1832, or his son, Alfio De Grassi, a mason and merchant who was well known in Toronto in the 1870s. Phillipe De Grassi was born in Italy and served with the French army in Spain, and then the British army in the West Indies. He lived in England for 16 years, making his living teaching languages, and immigrated to Canada to become a farmer. He had no experience or knowledge of farming, and a series of disasters and bad luck plagued him, including a fire that burned his house down and forced him to live in a stable for a time with his family. His property, where he built a sawmill and house, was located near the forks of the Don River, where Taylor Creek Park is today. De Grassi's daughter, Cornelia, who was 13 at the time, had an adventure in connection with the Rebellion of 1837. When De Grassi heard of the planned attack by the rebels, he rode to town with his two teenage daughters, Cornelia and Charlotte, to offer his support to Sir Francis Bond Head, the Lieutenant Governor. Cornelia then rode her horse up to where the rebels were gathered at Montgomery's Tavern, on Yonge St. north of Eglinton. She went to a wheelwright's shop nearby and spied on the rebels. They became suspicious and tried to stop her from leaving, but she galloped away and they shot at her, hitting her saddle and riding habit, but missing her. She rode back to Toronto and reported the numbers of rebels to Sir Francis, who then organized his troops to march on the rebels. The DeGrassi name lives on in the street name and in the name of a popular CBC-TV drama: *Degrassi Junior High*. See **BOND ST., MONTGOMERY AVE.**

DELISLE AVENUE

Yonge/St. Clair   Weymouth Schreiber bought some of Charles Heath's property in this area and subdivided it in 1874. He named one of the new streets after his wife, Harriet De Lisle of Guernsey. She was descended from Sir John De Lisle, who was Governor of Guernsey under Henry IV. Schreiber lived in a home on the south side of St. Clair Ave. West. Many years later his house was occupied by the Granite Club. See **DEER PARK CRESCENT.**

DENISON AVENUE

Dundas/Spadina   The Denisons were an influential family in York and Toronto in the 19th century, and their names and the names of their family connections can be traced in many street names. Captain John Denison (1757–1824), originally from Headon County, in Yorkshire, came to Upper Canada with his wife, Sophia, in the early 1800s, encouraged by their friends the Russells. Peter Russell was the first Administrator of York. When they first arrived, the Denisons lived in Castle Frank for a time, and then in 1804 Denison worked as Russell's farm manager at his estate, Petersfield. Denison began accumulating land. He had a farm on the Humber River and some land at the northwest corner of Queen and Ossington, where he built Brookfield House. He also acquired the lot next to Russell's, where his son George Taylor Denison (1783–1853) built Belle Vue. Denison Ave. was originally the drive up to this house. See **BELLEVUE AVE., BROOKFIELD ST., DOVERCOURT RD., HEYDON PARK RD., LIPPINCOTT ST., PETER ST., RUSHOLME DR.**

Great-grandsons of John Denison, circa 1877, from left to right: Frederick Charles, Henry Tyrwhitt, George Taylor III, Septimus Julius Augustus, John, Egerton Edmund Augustus and Clarence Alfred Kinsey Denison.

DEWSON STREET

College/Dovercourt
See **RUSHOLME DR.**

DINNICK CRESCENT

Mount Pleasant/Lawrence   Wilfred Servington Dinnick (1875–1923) was the president of Standard Loan and Company, a mortgage and loan company in Toronto. Dinnick planned Lawrence Park as a garden suburb, which was a popular new style of land development in England in the first decade of the century. The idea was to create a suburb for upper middle-class families, where the houses and gardens harmonized with the landscape. The plan, designed by English engineer W.S. Brooke, incorporated generous lots of 50 by 100 feet, winding crescents, circles and cul-de-sacs. The lots were carefully landscaped with a number of attractive features: terraces, summer houses, bridges, rockeries, croquet lawns, shrubberies and trees. Only houses were built: schools and shops were all outside the main residential area. In 1913 Dinnick instituted a Backyard Garden Competition across Toronto to boost the image of the garden suburb. When the First World War began the following year, the competition encouraged backyard vegetable gardens. During the war, Dinnick raised huge amounts of money for the Red Cross and the Toronto and York Patriotic Fund, and served as major in the 109th Regiment, which functioned chiefly as a supply and recruitment regiment. His business went bankrupt in 1919 and he died in 1923. See **LAWRENCE AVE.**

Construction of one of the first houses in Lawrence Park, circa 1911.

Sales office for Lawrence Park Estate, circa 1911.

Advertisement for Lawrence Park homes, white circles indicate houses already built.

DONALDA CRESCENT

Midland/Sheppard   Donalda Farms was a model dairy farm and property belonging to David A. Dunlap (1863–1924), a multi-millionaire involved in mining and finance. Born on a farm in Pembroke, Ontario, Dunlap practised law in Mattawa and spent his summers prospecting in northern Ontario. In 1903 he teamed up with Henry and Noah Timmins, owners of the general store in Mattawa, and started a silver mine in Cobalt. They discovered gold in Timmins in 1909 and later owned part of Hollinger and Noranda mines. In 1914 Dunlap and his wife, Jesse Donalda Bell, bought 800 acres east of the Don River, south of York Mills Rd., where he built Donalda Farms. He leased another 100 acres and created a modern dairy farm, with 40 buildings, 100 employees, Guernsey cattle and Clydesdale horses. The farm was exceedingly clean, with scrubbed, white-tiled barns where the animals were regularly vacuumed. Classical music was piped into the farm buildings. Dunlap built a Norman-style house on a hill, which resembled an English manor with beamed ceilings and a huge fireplace in the dining room. Terraces overlooked a heated swimming pool. The Toronto Hunt Club used his grounds for their activities. He contributed to Toronto General Hospital, Victoria University and the Art Gallery, and at his death in 1924 he was worth six million dollars. His hobby had been astronomy, so his wife gave the University of Toronto money in 1935 to build the David Dunlap Observatory, due north of the city. His home is today the clubhouse of the Donalda Golf and Country Club.

DOUVILLE COURT

Front/Parliament   Captain Alexandre Dagneau Douville (1698–1774) was a fur trader, soldier and interpreter in eastern Canada and the United States in the 18th century. In 1716 Alexandre and his brother, Jean, made their first visit to the future site of Toronto, where they travelled to the *fond du lac* ("bottom of the lake") to trade with the Iroquois. By 1720 they had established the first European Trading Post near the mouth of the Humber River. There is some confusion as to which Douville did what, since there were many of them with similar names and the records were not clear. Some sources suggest that this same Alexandre Douville, who became a captain in the French army, was in charge of Fort Toronto in 1759 when the French burned it down. In 1763 Douville was accused of misconduct because of illicit trade and banished from

Paris, although he didn't live in France at the time in question. This street was named in the same competition in 1979 that named Albert Franck Place, Henry Lane Terrace, Longboat Ave., Portneuf Court and Scadding Ave.

DOVERCOURT ROAD

Dufferin/Queen   Dover Court was the home built in 1853 at the northwest corner of Dundas and Ossington by Richard Lippincott Denison (1814–78), the eldest son of George Taylor Denison (1783–1853). Richard grew up at Belle Vue and married Susan Hepbourne in 1837, when he built the first Dover Court. In 1853 he built a larger house with wide verandahs. His grandmother, Sophia Taylor Denison, lived at Brookfield, south of his estate. He named his house after her home in Essex, England. Lakeview Ave. was the carriage drive that led to his house. Colonel Denison was active in the Toronto Militia and bred cavalry horses. Dover Court was demolished in 1933 and Hepbourne St. was named after his wife. See **BELLEVUE AVE., BROOKFIELD ST., DENISON AVE., HEYDON PARK RD., RUSHOLME DR.**

DRAPER STREET

Front/Spadina   William Henry Draper (1801–77) had a long and distinguished political career. His eloquence earned him the nickname "Sweet William." When he first came to Canada from England he taught school in Port Hope. Draper was called to the bar in 1828 and elected to the legislature in 1836. In 1837 he was appointed Solicitor General of Canada, and then Attorney General in 1841. Draper led the Conservatives in the provincial government between 1841 and 1847. From 1863 to 1869 he was Chief Justice of Upper Canada, and then served as president on the Court of Error and Appeals in Ontario from 1869 until his death in 1877.

DRUMSNAB ROAD

Bayview/Bloor   Drumsnab was the name of a house built overlooking the Don Valley in 1834 by Francis Cayley. He took the name from a house in a Sir Walter Scott novel. In Northern English dialect, a drumsnab was a cone of sugar, called a sugarloaf. Special sugar nippers were used to snip off bits of sugar. If you visit the basement kitchen of the Grange, which has been restored to its 19th century condition, you can see sugar loaves and even cut off some sugar with antique sugar nippers. Sugarloaf Hill was a sharp, triangular hill standing about where the Prince Edward Viaduct now joins the western side of the Don Valley. Cayley's house overlooked it; hence its name. Francis Cayley was an artist and architect, and he built his single-storey house from fieldstone with two-foot thick walls, twelve-foot ceilings and a wide verandah. A second storey was added in 1850. Cayley decorated the dining room walls and doors with murals depicting scenes from *Faust* and *Don Quixote*. In the hall he painted a clever *trompe l'oeil* of a hatrack with his cloak,

Drumsnab, the oldest inhabited building in Toronto.

hat and walking stick hanging from it, with a note written underneath: "As long as Drumsnab stands my hat and cloak will hang in the front hall." Drumsnab still stands, and Francis Cayley's hat and cloak still hang at 5 Drumsnab Rd. It is the oldest inhabited building in Toronto. See **GRANGE AVE., WAVERLEY RD.**

DUFFERIN STREET

CNE grounds to Steeles between Bathurst and Roncesvalles/Keele   Until the 1880s, Dufferin St., known then as the Side Line, was the western boundary of the city. In 1876 the street was named after the Governor General of the time, Frederick Temple Blackwood (1826–1902), Lord Dufferin. Dufferin was an accomplished linguist (Latin, Greek, French, Persian and Italian)

After a happy day at the CNE, visitors leave by the resplendent Dufferin Gates in the 1920s.

who had been educated at Eton and Oxford. In the course of his career he served as Lord-in-Waiting to Queen Victoria, Under-Secretary for India from 1864 to 1866, Governor General of Canada from 1872 to 1878, Ambassador to St. Petersburg between 1869 and 1882 and Viceroy of India in 1884. While in Canada he travelled to the Arctic by canoe and to British Columbia by horseback. He opened the first Canadian National Exhibition in 1878. See **WITHROW AVE.**

DUNCANMILL ROAD

Don Mills/York Mills   Duncan Mill Rd. draws its name from the mills owned by David Duncan in the 18th century. William Duncan was the earliest settler in the area of Sheppard Ave. and Dufferin St. In 1848 he purchased two lots in the Don Mills Rd./York Mills Rd. area. The lot south of York Mills he gave to his son Henry, who later became a reeve of York Township. In 1873 he gave the other lot to his son David, who had just married Anne Laird. David became a well-respected dairy farmer, known for breeding fine Jersey cows. He called his farm Moatfield. A devastating flood of the Don River in 1878 destroyed his mills and his original house, but they were rebuilt, and when he died he left his farm to his son Gordon.

DUNDAS STREET

Kingston Rd. to Dixie between Queen/Queensway and Danforth/Bloor (hops north of Bloor between Roncesvalles and Kipling)   Dundas St. was named after the Right Honourable Henry Dundas (1742–1811), Viscount Melville, who was Home Secretary from 1791 to 1794 when Simcoe began building Dundas Rd. Melville held prominent positions in three different British governments and often had dealings with issues related to North America. He also served as the Lord Advocate for Scotland, effectively ruling that country for 30 years. Dundas Rd. was originally part of Lord Simcoe's plan for a great highway from Detroit through London and York to Kingston. The eastern section of the highway became Kingston Rd., while the western section was slowly completed over the course of the 18th century. When Simcoe laid out the town of York, Detroit was in British hands. Simcoe wanted to build Dundas Rd. as a military road in case of war with the Americans. Dundas St. has incorporated many smaller streets over the years.

A streetcar crosses the intersection at Bloor and Dundas St. W. in 1927.

Traffic police display their fine fleet of motorcycles on Dundas St. near University in 1928.

DUNN AVENUE

Dufferin/King   This street was named after John Henry Dunn (1792–1854), a businessman, politician and officer in the militia, who served as the Receiver General of Upper Canada between 1820 and 1843. During this time he bought much of the land south of Queen between Roncesvalles and Cowan that eventually became the village of Parkdale. The land was subdivided in 1873, when Dunn St. was named. Dunn's son, Alexander Robert Dunn (1833–68), a war hero who fought in the Crimean War, was the first Canadian to win the Victoria Cross. He won it for his part in the Charge of the Light Brigade in the battle of Balaclava when he was only 21. Since Dunn Jr. was a graduate of Upper Canada College, his medal has been kept by the school.

DUPONT STREET

Avenue Rd./Davenport
See **DAVENPORT RD.**

EDGAR AVENUE

Mount Pleasant/St. Clair   There are two possible sources for the name of this street. One is Edgar Jarvis, the nephew of Sheriff William Botsford Jarvis (1799–1864), who was involved in the development of the Rosedale estate (which had belonged to Sheriff Jarvis) after it was subdivided in 1853. Edgar Jarvis built homes in the area, including Glenhurst and Sylvan Towers. However, there is a slightly stronger case for the other Edgar, Sir James David Edgar (1841–99), who was the Speaker of the House of Commons. Sir James Edgar, a lawyer, journalist and poet, was involved in politics for many years, first as a member of the Reform party and then as a Liberal. He was strong on organization and finance, and was made Speaker in 1896. Some of the streets in this area were named in 1907 when they were laid out by the Scottish Ontario and Manitoba Land Co., and there is a strong suggestion that the street was named after Sir James. See **HIGHLAND AVE.**

EGLINTON AVENUE

Kingston to Dixie between Danforth/Bloor and Lawrence   The source of the name Eglinton, the village and then the street, is somewhat murky. The area around Yonge and Eglinton began to be settled after the war of 1812, when veterans of that conflict were granted land there. John Montgomery, whose tavern here was burned down in the Rebellion of 1837, was said to have been related to the Scottish Montgomerys who were the Earls of Eglinton. He may have drawn the name for the area from his ancestors. Or it may have been named by veterans who settled here after the War of 1812. Their patron was the 12th Earl of Eglinton, Hugh Montgomerie (1740–1819), who was a Colonel in the West Lowland Fencibles during the Seven Years War. Or it

CTA SC 244 Item 508

Eglinton west of Yonge in the 1920s had a sidewalk and hydro lines, but few houses.

could have been named after Eglinton Castle. The 13th Earl of Eglinton, Archibald William Montgomerie (1812–61), was famous for a huge field tournament he organized at Eglinton Castle near Prestwick, England, in 1839, where knights jousted in medieval style. Louis Napoleon was one of the knights, and the affair was famous throughout the world, not least because of its great expense: between £30,000 and £40,000. Whatever the source of the name, Eglinton had grown into a village with a post office by 1856. The village was eventually swallowed up by North Toronto, which was annexed to Toronto in 1912. See **MONTGOMERY AVE.**

ELGIN STREET

Avenue Rd./Bloor   James Bruce (1811–63), the 8th Earl of Elgin, was the son of Thomas Bruce, the 7th Earl of Elgin, who brought the Elgin Marbles from Greece to Britain in 1816. They're still in the British Museum. James studied at Eton and Oxford and for a time served as a Conservative Member of Parliament in England. In 1842 he went to Jamaica as Governor, and there he displayed his diplomatic and administrative skills while coping with the aftermath of the abolition of slavery. In 1847 he came to Canada as Governor General and was instrumental in settling some of the outstanding issues of the day. He supported the Rebellion Losses Bill in 1849, which compensated people who had property damaged in the 1837 Rebellion. Opposition to this was so fierce that he was pelted with eggs and stones. After he left Canada in 1854, Elgin went on to China and later served as the Viceroy and Governor General of India.

ELM GROVE

Dufferin/King
See **GWYNNE AVE.**

ELMSLEY PLACE

Bay/Wellesley   This small street is a private road on the University of Toronto campus. It commemorates Captain John Elmsley (1801–63), a devout converted Catholic who sailed the Great Lakes and named many of the streets in this area after Catholic saints. His father was Chief Justice of Upper Canada, John Elmsley (1762–1805). John Jr. grew up in England after his father's death and joined the Royal Navy in 1815, where he remained until 1824. He came to Upper Canada in 1825 to manage his father's land. Elected to the Executive Council and the Legislative Council, Elmsley soon became a prominent figure in the community. He married a Catholic, Charlotte Sherwood, in 1831 with two ceremonies: one wedding was at St. Paul's Catholic Church and the other was held at the Anglican St. James. Soon afterwards Captain Elmsley converted to Catholicism and remained a staunch supporter of the Catholic Church all his life. He was a great advocate of separate schools and served as a school trustee for a time. His house, Clover Hill, stood on the hill near the northeast corner of Bay and Joseph streets, near the spot where Elmsley Place is today. Elmsley commanded a boat during the Rebellion of 1837, and then in 1841 was the captain of the steamer *Cobourg*, which sailed between Kingston, Cobourg, Port Hope and Toronto. He later was the captain of the *Niagara*, another steamer. Elmsley generously gave land and money to the Catholic church and institutions, such as the Sisters of St. Joseph. He donated the land where St. Michael's College and St. Basil's Church were built. Streets in the area reflect his adopted faith: St. Mary, St. Joseph, St. Nicholas, St. Thomas and St. Vincent. When he died he left instructions for his body to be buried in St. Michael's Cathedral and his heart to be tucked away in the wall of St. Basil's Church.

EUCLID AVENUE

Bathurst/Dundas   Why this street was called Euclid is not clear, but its namesake is the Greek mathematician who lived in Greece in approximately 300 B.C. He wrote the famous text, *Elements* (of geometry), which took up 13 books and has been used in some form as a basic math book for centuries, including the early 20th century. He wrote many other books on geometry, astronomy and music, but most of them have been lost.

FARADAY DRIVE

Ellesmere/McCowan   It is possible that this street was named after Michael Faraday (1791–1867), who is considered the greatest of experimental physicists. He gained his education as the assistant to Humphrey Davy, and in 1827 took over the Chair of Chemistry at the Royal Institute, a prestigious scientific organization in London, England. His many accomplishments included the isolation of benzene, the discovery of electromagnetic induction, the laws of electrolysis, and the rotation of polarized light by magnetism. He published his findings over 40 years in a work named *Experimental Researches on Electricity*, and his experiments and writing had a great influence on the study of physics. See **SPENCER AVE., TYNDALL AVE.**

FARNHAM AVENUE

St. Clair/Yonge   Farnham Lodge was the name of a house built in 1844 by a successful pharmacist, Edward Hooper (1808–1900). Hooper grew up in Surrey, England, and he named his house after his boyhood home. After training as a chemist in England, Hooper came to Canada in 1832 and in 1838 settled in Toronto, where he worked for Beckett's Chemist Shop at King and Yonge. He eventually bought the company and E. Hooper & Co. grew to be a chain of eight drugstores. Hooper bought six acres between Avenue Rd. and Yonge St. and built his house and farm there. The house and coach house still survive. The property was sold in 1899, and the new owner, John Blackwell, worked out a deal with a neighbour (Dr. Armstrong) and the city, whereby each of them donated 33 feet of land to the city to build a public street to lead to their properties. The street was named Farnham, after Hooper's house.

FERMANAGH AVENUE

Dundas/Roncesvalles
See **O'HARA AVE.**

FINCH AVENUE

Morningside to Steeles between Sheppard and Steeles   This street was named after John Finch, who built an inn at the corner of Finch and Yonge in 1847. Before Finch bought the property, it was owned by John Montgomery, who later owned the famous Montgomery Tavern at Eglinton and Yonge that was burned down in the Rebellion of 1837. In about 1820 John and his father, Alexander Montgomery, built an inn on the northern property, which they called the Bird-in-the-Hand. After a dispute in 1827, they had the house legally divided and then sawed in half! Alexander lived in the northern part of the house, and John lived in the southern part, which he continued to

At the Bird-in-the Hand tavern John Finch specialized in fine cooking. Circa 1848.

operate as an inn. When he built his new inn near Eglinton and Yonge in the 1830s, he leased the Bird-in-the-Hand to John Finch. Finch bought the property in 1847 and built a new two-storey frame hotel. The hotel was known for its good cooking, and in 1851 Finch arranged for a travelling circus to perform on his property. See **MONTGOMERY AVE.**

FLEMING DRIVE

Bayview/Finch   Although there is no direct proof, this street may have been named after Sir Sandford Fleming (1827–1915), a railway surveyor, construction engineer and the inventor of Standard Time. Fleming was born in Scotland and came to Canada in 1845. In 1863 he was appointed a railway surveyor by the Canadian government, and from that date until 1880 he worked on surveys of proposed railway routes across Canada. Some of his suggestions were followed; others were rejected. Fleming was involved in various other projects, including the proposal to lay a telecommunications cable from Canada to Australia. The Pacific Cable was finally completed in 1902. One of Fleming's major and longest lasting contributions to the world was his invention of Standard Time. He devised the system that divided the world into 24 time zones, and he organized the Prime Meridian Conference in Washington in 1884, where the system was adopted. It was for this achievement he was knighted in 1897 by Queen Victoria. Fleming owned land north of Lawrence Ave. between Keele and Jane.

FOXLEY PLACE
FOXLEY STREET

Ossington/Queen   Foxley Grove was the name of the house in Berkshire, England, where Samuel Bealey Harrison (1802–67) grew up. A lawyer, he made a name for himself in England as the author of a series of books called *Harrison's Digests*, which were a compilation of important cases heard in the House of Lords. He retired from law because of illness and came to Canada in 1837. He bought land near Oakville, where he built a sawmill and a grist mill. But skilled lawyers with his experience were rare in Upper Canada and he was called back into the world of politics and law in 1839, when he was appointed the civil secretary to the Lieutenant Governor of the time, Sir George Arthur.

Harrison swiftly became involved in the politics of the time, supporting the Reformers and responsible government. He was the government leader in the assembly for four years and was appointed provincial secretary for Canada West on the Executive Council in 1841. He had a profound influence on politics in Upper Canada during his short involvement, and was known for his clear head and gift for analysis. In 1845 he was made a judge and he retired from active politics. From 1852 Harrison lived in Foxley Grove on Dundas St. with his second wife, Ellen Humphreys. Harrison loved gardening and nurtured many exotic plants in his conservatory and grounds.

FRIZZEL ROAD

Sheppard/Yonge   There is some question as to whether this road was named after a preacher, William Frizzell, who lived in the area and in 1882 was made the pastor of Queen Street Presbyterian Church, or Richard Frizzell, a young man who had a significant role in the Rebellion of 1837. The name lost an "l" at some point. Robertson's *Landmarks* gives a lively account of Richard Frizzell's adventures over the course of December 4, 5 and 6, 1837. First his mother hid his pants to keep him from going out and getting into trouble. When he finally escaped from her, he learned of the rebels gathering and tried to get a horse to ride to Toronto to warn the Governor, but no one would lend him one. He finally walked all the way from north of Eglinton down to City Hall. Sir Francis Bond Head refused at first to believe him, suspecting he was in the employ of the rebels and spreading false information. In the end Sir Francis was convinced of his honesty and Frizzell joined the Loyalists marching north against the rebels.

FROBISHER AVENUE

St.Clair/Yonge   Sir Martin Frobisher (1535 or 1539–1594) was a pirate, an explorer and a war hero who was knighted for his part in the war against the Spanish Armada with Sir Francis Drake in 1588. Frobisher set out in 1576 to find the fabled Northwest Passage that would lead Europeans past the continent of North America to the wealth of the Orient. He actually thought he had reached China when he discovered Frobisher Bay. He returned to England with a captured Inuit he insisted was a Chinese man, and some ore he thought might contain gold. He led two more expeditions to find gold but the ore was eventually proved to have no value. His disgrace was mitigated 10 years later when he fought against the Spanish Armada with Drake. He died after being wounded in a battle against the Spanish near Brest, France, in 1594. Although he really didn't know where he was and left behind no accurate account of his explorations, he is considered one of the important explorers who searched for the Northwest Passage.

FRONT STREET

Bayview to Bathurst between Lake Shore Blvd. and King   When the town of York was laid out by Governor John Graves Simcoe in 1793, Front St. was the street that ran along the lakefront. The eastern portion was first named King St., after George III (b. 1738, r. 1760–1820), and later Palace St., because it led to the Parliament Buildings at the foot of Berkeley St. Now it is all Front St., but lies at some distance from the lakefront, since landfill, highways and harbourfront development have extended the city into what used to be the harbour.

NAC C-040137

York, Upper Canada, 1804. Elizabeth Frances Hale painted this early view of Front St., with the Parliament buildings on the far right.

The Dominion Public Building curves gently along the south side of Front St. between Yonge and Bay, 1955.

GARDINER EXPRESSWAY

Leslie to Hwy 427 between Lake Shore Blvd. and Queen/Queensway   Frederick Goldwin Gardiner (1895–1983) was the first chairman of the newly formed Metro Toronto, from 1953 to 1961. His personality and policies had a major impact on the city. He hired the staff and directed the policies that made Metro Council function. He pushed construction projects through aggressively and was the major force behind the creation of the Gardiner

Expressway, begun in 1955 and finally completed in 1966. The highway was named in his honour in 1957, while he was still in office. Gardiner was known for being aggressive and getting things done, but he also had the political skill to work effectively with the various factions in city and provincial government. He retired from Council in 1961 and from 1965 to 1979 served as Hydro Commissioner.

GEOFFREY STREET

Dundas/Roncesvalles
See **O'HARA AVE.**

GEORGE STREET

Jarvis/Queen This street was named in 1793 when York was first laid out, after the Prince of Wales, who later became George IV (b. 1762, r. 1820–30). George was an interesting character who loved to eat, drink and pursue women, and at one point had two wives at the same time. His first wife was a Roman Catholic widow, Maria Anne Fitzherbert (1756–1837), whom he married secretly in a Catholic ceremony without his father's consent in 1785. This marriage was later declared invalid under the Royal Marriage Act of 1772. In 1795 the Prince made a political marriage to his first cousin, Caroline Brunswick of Wolfenbüttel (1768–1821) to appease Parliament and get his debts paid off. Although they had a daughter, they never got along and Caroline lived apart from him. When he succeeded to the throne in 1820, Caroline refused an offer to buy her off and renounce her title, and returned to London to claim her position as Queen. George responded by charging her with adultery. The public supported her and the charges were dropped. She died soon afterwards. George went on to rule the country. Nobody has much good to say about this king: he spread rumours about his father's insanity when George III fell ill in 1788. However, he was capable, when sober, of being amusing and clever and had considerable talent as a comic. Apparently he was a man of culture, much more intelligent than any other members of the Hanover line, and he left the country his substantial collection of books and paintings. See **BRUNSWICK AVE.**

GIBSON AVENUE

Yonge/Davenport   This street was possibly named after David Gibson (1804–64), the city of Toronto's first City Surveyor (1834) and a major figure in the Rebellion of 1837. Gibson lived with his family in a house he built on the west side of Yonge St. north of Sheppard. He was elected to the Legislative Assembly twice as an avid member of the Reform Party, led by William Lyon Mackenzie. During the short-lived Rebellion, Gibson was in charge of the Tory prisoners, and when the Loyalist army was approaching Montgomery's Tavern, he led the prisoners up the hill on Yonge St. to about where Lawrence Park stands today. There he let them go and managed to escape himself. He hid in a haystack for a few weeks at a friend's house near Oshawa, waiting for a boat to take him across the lake to the United States. He finally made it across and settled in Lockport, where he found work as an engineer on the Erie Canal. His house was burned down by the Loyalists in the aftermath of the Rebellion, and his family joined him later in Lockport, where they remained until 1848. Gibson was then given a full pardon and returned to Canada, where he built another house that still stands today. It has been made into a museum and restored to its original state. Gibson returned to his career as a surveyor and later became Inspector of Crown Land Agencies and Superintendent of Colonization Roads for Canada West.

GIVINS STREET

Ossington/Queen   Colonel James Givins (1784–1842) built his substantial home, Pine Grove, in 1802 near the corner of today's Queen and Givins. Givins (sometimes spelled Givens) was made a lieutenant in the Queen's Rangers under Governor Simcoe. He is known to have led an expedition up Goodwin's Creek, mistakenly believing it to be the Don River. Givins learned the Ojibwa language and other First Nations dialects and served as interpreter for Simcoe. Givins was made the Assistant Superintendent of Indian Affairs, and he clashed with Joseph Brant over Brant's attempt to organize a widespread Native organization. In the American invasion in April 1813, Givins, now a major in the militia, led a small group of

Mississaugas to try to defend York, but they were outnumbered. After the war, Givins continued in his post as Superintendent of Indian Affairs, and he helped to establish a mission village on the Credit River, which eventually became the model for the reserve system. His house, which was torn down in 1891, was famous for the dreadful bloodstains under the carpet in the drawing room. Legend had it that the blood was that of Natives and soldiers in the battle of 1813. Angelica Givins, James' wife, was known for her surgical skill in treating their battle wounds, and apparently the drawing room served as the operating area.

TRL T 11238 JRR

The dreadful bloodstains under the rug at Pine Grove were souvenirs of the American invasion in 1813. Circa 1888.

GLADSTONE AVENUE

Dufferin/Dundas   William Ewart Gladstone (1809–98) was a prominent English statesman who was elected Prime Minister four times. He started out in Parliament in 1832 as a Tory under then-Prime Minister Sir Robert Peel, who first appointed him a junior Lord of the Treasury and then later the Under-Secretary for the Colonies. In subsequent Peel governments Gladstone held several other important positions, but he finally switched allegiance to the Liberal party as a matter of conscience concerning what he considered the injustices perpetuated by the social system in Britain. He served as Chancellor of the Exchequer and then became the leader of the House of Commons. In 1868 he was elected Prime Minister. Gladstone was famous for his skilled oratory and gave impassioned and eloquent speeches in the House. He and Disraeli, the Conservative leader who was also Prime Minister during this period, maintained a fierce rivalry. Among his many accomplishments as Prime Minister, Gladstone supported the introduction of a national education system, passed a bill to improve the rights of Irish tenants, and presided over the disestablishment of the Irish church. He advocated Home Rule for Ireland but was ultimately defeated in this by the House of Lords.

GLEN AMES

Queen/Woodbine
See **GLEN MANOR DR.**

GLEN EDYTH DRIVE
GLEN EDYTH PLACE

Davenport/Spadina   Glen Edyth was the name of the estate built by Samuel Nordheimer in 1872, very near where Glen Edyth Dr. runs today. He took his inspiration for the name of his house from his wife, Edith Louise Boulton, and a picturesque glen on his property. It was a grand and beautiful house with a long drive leading to it through a charming landscaped estate, featuring rustic bridges, a waterfall, a duck pond, summer houses and a kitchen garden, all reminiscent of an English country manor. With 35 rooms, towers, turrets and a widow's walk, the house was known as one of the finest in Toronto. Samuel Nordheimer and his brother Abraham were members of a wealthy Jewish family of Bavarian merchants. They came first to New York in 1839 and then to Kingston in 1841. They began a business importing musical instruments from Europe and started manufacturing pianos. It grew into a very successful enterprise with branches in Montreal, Kingston, Hamilton and London. They moved their headquarters to Toronto in the early 1860s. Samuel also had business interests in various financial institutions. He converted to Anglicanism in 1871, married Edith Boulton, and bought the property where he would build his lovely home. They entertained lavishly, holding balls, receptions, weddings and musical performances. The house was demolished in 1929. See **BOULTON AVE.**

GLENGROVE AVENUE

Bathurst/Lawrence   Glengrove was the name James Beaty (1807–83) gave to his summer home. He bought the farm from the Nanton family, who had called it "The Pilgrims." The property was known for its impressive avenue of pines, which remained along Glengrove Ave. for many years. James Beaty, a shoemaker born in Ireland, came to York in 1818 where he established a boot-making shop. He traded in leather and had some success with buying and selling real estate. He served as a councilman in 1836 and an alderman in 1846. A staunch supporter of the Reform party, he put out a newspaper, the *Toronto Leader*, between 1852 and 1878. For many years it represented the Liberal-Conservative viewpoint in Upper Canada. Leader Lane, in downtown Toronto near King and Yonge streets, was named after this newspaper, which had its offices there. In 1867 and 1872 Beaty won a Conservative seat in the House of Commons. There was one major scandal associated with Beaty, known as the York Road Job. Using his influence with politicians, he bought three toll-roads leading into the city for what was considered a ridiculously low sum of money. He never actually made much money on his investment, and by 1863 the roads reverted back to the province's ownership, but a great stink was raised at the time in all directions.

In the mid-1920s the rows of tall pines from the original farm still stood proudly along Glengrove Ave.

GLEN MANOR DRIVE
GLEN STEWART AVENUE
GLEN STEWART CRESCENT

Queen/Woodbine   Glen Stewart was the name of an estate that occupied about 28 acres in the Beach area of Toronto from 1872 to the early 1900s. Its boundaries were from Lee Ave on the west to Beech on the east, between Queen St. and Kingston Rd. The property was bought in 1872 by William Stewart Darling (1818–88), an Anglican minister who had been appointed to the Parish of Scarborough in 1843 and served at the Church of the Holy Trinity in downtown Toronto from 1843 to 1882. Darling built the house and named it Glen Stewart. It was sold in 1900 to Alfred Ernest Ames (1866–1934), a wealthy stockbroker. He used it as a summer home for a time, building additions and making improvements. Then he moved there permanently to enjoy country living: the trout pond, the landscaped grounds, the quaint bridges, the beautiful ravines and the golf course. He opened his property to the local public, letting them use the golf course and enjoy the grounds with picnics, hiking parties, skating and sleighing. The house is noted for its illustrious occupant in 1905 and 1906: Governor General Earl Grey used it as his official residence for the month of May in each of those years. The land was subdivided and developed, starting in 1910. In 1931 the ravine was given to the city for a park, Glen Stewart Park. The house was divided into apartments but still stands, and many streets in the area echo the name of the estate and its owners: Glen Manor Dr., Glen Stewart Crescent, and Glen Ames.

GORE STREET
GORE VALE AVENUE

Bathurst/Dundas   Gore Vale was the name of a 100-acre lot granted to Captain Samuel Smith in 1806 that stretched from Queen to Bloor, including the land where Trinity-Bellwoods Park now stands. Smith named it after Sir Francis Gore (1769–1852), the Lieutenant Governor of Upper Canada from 1806 to 1817. Garrison Creek ran through the property at the bottom of a ravine, which inspired the "Vale" part of the name (both the ravine and the creek were eventually paved over). Sir Francis Gore was most famous for his last act as Lieutenant Governor: in 1817, after trouble with the Legislative Assembly, he cancelled all its meetings and returned to England. Smith never built on the property, but Duncan Cameron, a member of the Legislative Assembly and the Provincial Secretary and Registrar, bought it and in 1820 built a three-storey brick house there, keeping the name Gore Vale. In 1849 part of the property was sold to Bishop Strachan in trust for Trinity College (built in 1851). The house was bought in 1870 by Edward Oscar Brickford, the president of the Erie and Huron Railway, who named two of the nearby streets after his daughters, Grace and Beatrice. Over the years the house passed to various owners, and at one time was the home of the Keeley Institute, where alcoholics were treated. Later it became a residence for Trinity College, until it was demolished in 1926. Students of modern American politics have enjoyed the coincidence that Gore St. crosses Clinton just south of College. See **STRACHAN AVE., TRINITY CIRCLE.**

Gore Vale stood for over a hundred years near Trinity Park, north of Queen St. Circa 1900.

GRACE STREET

Dundas/Ossington
See **GORE VALE AVE.**

GRAND OPERA LANE

King/Yonge   The Grand Opera House, at 9-15 Adelaide St. West, opened on September 21, 1874. One of the main venues for visiting troupes and local productions of opera and theatre, it played host to many 19th century celebrities, including Oscar Wilde, Sarah Bernhardt and Henry Irving. It burned down on November 28, 1879, after a production of that very unlucky play,

Macbeth. The walls were left standing and it was quickly rebuilt, opening for a performance of *Romeo and Juliet* just a few weeks later, on February 9, 1880. In the early 20th century the Grand Opera House slowly declined, due to competition from newer theatres (the Royal Alexandra and the Princess). It was a vaudeville house for a while, then a movie house and was finally demolished in 1927. In 1919 one of Toronto's greatest unsolved mysteries began just outside the Opera House. Ambrose Small, who had owned it since 1903, disappeared on December 2, 1919, after depositing a huge amount of money ($1.5 million) in his bank account. He was last seen walking away from the Grand Opera House, and no one has ever discovered what happened to him.

The Grand Opera House was gutted by fire after an extremely unlucky performance of *Macbeth* in 1879. Circa 1875.

GRANGE AVENUE

Dundas/Spadina "The Grange" was the name D'Arcy Boulton Jr. (1785–1846) gave to the handsome Georgian house he built in 1820 on his country estate, which lay between today's McCaul and Beverley streets. It was then quite isolated from the town of York, surrounded by thick forest. He built a beautifully proportioned Georgian home, set in a park with a circular drive-way. Orchards, cricket and lacrosse fields, and a racetrack were established on his land, and over the years the house had many improvements, including an orangery and a library. His son, William Henry Boulton (1812–74), was mayor of Toronto and lived in the house after his father's death. The house was left to William Boulton's widow, Harriette Mann Dixon, who married Goldwin Smith (1823–1910) in 1875. Smith, a historian and journalist, was known for

Guests enjoy a leisurely game of croquet on the lawn of the Grange, circa 1867.

his firm conviction that Canada would never survive as a country and should be annexed to the United States. When Harriette died in 1911, she left the house to the Art Museum of Toronto, which evolved into the Art Gallery of Ontario. One of the oldest remaining houses in Toronto, the Grange was restored in the 1970s to a living museum, where visitors can experience how the upper classes lived in Toronto in the 1830s. It is situated due south of the Art Gallery of Ontario, connected to the modern building by an atrium. See **DRUMSNAB RD., BOULTON AVE.**

GRAYDON HALL DRIVE

Don Mills/York Mills   Graydon Hall was the name of a 29-room Georgian manor built by Henry Rupert Bain (1898–1952) in 1936, just east of the Don River and north of York Mills Rd. The name may have been a combination of "gray" and "don," referring to James Gray, who had operated mills on the Don River. Henry Bain made his fortune as a broker handling mining finance and bought the 100-acre property, formerly farmland, in 1934. Graydon Hall had spectacular formal gardens with waterfalls and a tea pavilion. There were stables for Bain's polo ponies and hunters, kennels for the dogs he raised, and a 10-car garage. An intriguing story surrounds his divorce: his ex-wife married his friend Reginald Watkins in 1951, then a week later Bain married Watkins' ex-wife. When he died the next year, there was a lawsuit over which wife should inherit his estate. The first wife won. Graydon Hall is still there on Graydon Hall Drive, partially occupied and in a bad state of repair.

GREENSIDES AVENUE

Oakwood/St. Clair   The Greensides family owned a property between Atlas and Arlington, with a brickyard at the southern end on the portion between Benson and Tyrell. Isaac Greensides was born in Yorkshire and came to Canada in 1837, where he farmed and established a bricklaying company. His son William and grandson Henry continued in the brickmaking business on this property. The street was named after the Greensides in 1918.

GWYNNE AVENUE

Dufferin/Queen   In 1833 Dr. William Charles Gwynne (1806–75) bought just over 100 acres between Queen St. and the lake, and Dufferin and Cowan. Here he commissioned the architect John Howard to build a house, situated on the west side of Dufferin in between today's Thorburn and Temple avenues. Gwynne named it Elm Grove. Dr. Gwynne, who was born in Ireland, had immigrated to Canada in 1832 and shortly thereafter married into the influential Powell family. He practised medicine, taught anatomy and physiology at King's College (University of Toronto), and served on the commission that managed the Provincial Lunatic Asylum. In 1853 the university got rid of its medical school, and Gwynne, who was known as a man of strong opinions and fierce energy, was so furious with the decision that he left the country and went to live in Britain for three years. However, he returned to Canada in 1856 to live on his farm and study insects. Two years after his death in 1875 his daughter, Eliza Anne Gwynne, subdivided the land for development, keeping the area around the house for herself. She named three local streets after her father's favourite philosophers and scientists: Huxley (this street later became Springhurst Ave.), Tyndall and Spencer. A romantic story clung to Eliza Gywnne: she was said to have lost a fiancé in the Crimean war, and to have kept a large elm near her house so that each night she could revisit the spot where they used to meet. Whether or not this was true is hard to say, but Eliza Gwynne lived in Elm Grove and kept the farm going until her death in 1910. Her love for animals was reflected in her will: she left $75,000 to the Anti-Vivisection Society of England and $25,000 to the Toronto Humane Society. The developers moved in and the house was finally demolished in 1917. See **HOWARD PARK AVE., SPENCER AVE., TYNDALL AVE.**

HADRIAN DRIVE

Islington/Rexdale   The Emperor Hadrian (76–138) ruled over the vast Roman Empire from 117 to 138 C.E. He was the ward and protégé of the previous Emperor Trajan, who named Hadrian to succeed him after his death. Hadrian was a skilled administrator and military commander who undertook a long tour of his extensive empire between 120 and 126 C.E., travelling north through Europe to Britain and east through Egypt, Asia Minor and Greece. While in Britain he ordered the construction of Hadrian's Wall, a 117-km defensive wall from the Tyne River to Solway Firth, across the narrowest point of the island of Britain. Begun in 122 and completed in 126, parts of the wall and the stone blockhouses that were built along it remain today. Hadrian's Romanizing policy in Palestine and the exclusion of Jews from Jerusalem led to a rebellion led by Bar-Kokhba and a bitter war between 132 and 135. In Rome Hadrian reorganized the civil service, built several monuments and patronized the arts.

CTA SC 244 Item 129A

A pole painter enjoys a bird's-eye view of Front St. west of Yonge in 1907.

HAGERMAN STREET

Bay/Dundas   Christopher Alexander Hagerman (1792–1847) was a lawyer, politician and judge who served in the Assembly for four Parliaments as an outspoken representative of the Family Compact. He was Solicitor General from 1829 to 1833 and Attorney General from 1837 to 1840. A large, aggressive, impulsive man with a gift for oratory, he became a fierce opponent of the Reformers. Known as "Handsome Kit" in his youth, he was anointed with another nickname, "that great mastiff" by the writer Anna Brownell Jameson, who was apparently quite fond of him. See **JAMESON AVE.**

HALIBURTON AVENUE

Kipling/Rathburn   Thomas Chandler Haliburton (1796–1865) was born into a Nova Scotian family of Tory lawyers and judges. Admitted to the bar in 1820, Haliburton was a member of the Assembly by 1826 and a judge by 1829. He served on the Nova Scotia Supreme Court from 1855 to 1856, when he retired and moved to England. There he had a political career as a Tory Member of Parliament for six years. Over the course of his life he wrote books on history and politics, but he became Canada's first internationally famous author because of his humorous novels, in particular *The Clockmaker; or The Sayings and Doings of Samuel Slick of Slickville*. It ran as a series of instalments in the *Novascotian* newspaper and was first published as a book in 1836. This brilliant satire of Americans proved to be wildly popular on both sides of the Atlantic. Two of his later works were *The Old Judge; or Life in a Colony* (1849) and *Rule and Misrule of the English in Massachusetts* (1851). Haliburton was considered the Canadian Mark Twain. While living in England, Haliburton was the Chairman of a company based in London called the Canadian Land and Emigration Company. In 1861 he travelled to Ontario to buy a million acres in the area that was later named after him: Haliburton County.

HANNA ROAD

Bayview/Millwood   David Blythe Hanna (1858–1938) was a classic example of someone who worked his way up from the bottom of an industry to the top. He began as a ticket seller in Scotland at the age of 14, and would eventually become the first president of the Canadian National Railway in Canada. Starting with a position in the Audit Department of the Grand Trunk Railway in Manitoba in 1882, he worked for several railway companies in both Canada and the United States, and in 1896 joined up with Sir William Mackenzie and Sir Donald Mann, who were in the process of creating the Canada Northern Railway, the third transcontinental railway in the country. Hanna became vice-president in charge of operations. They chose the site of Leaside to establish a railway town, built up around railway yards and maintenance sheds. When the government bought their company, Hanna was appointed president of the board of directors of the new company, Canadian National Railway. His last official position was as the first chairman of the Liquor Control Board of Ontario from 1927 to 1928, a job he was persuaded to take after he retired. See **LEA AVE., LAIRD DR.**

HARRISON ROAD

Bayview/York Mills   William Harrison (1784–1838) was one of the casualties of the Rebellion of 1837. An ardent Reformer, he was wounded in the battle in December but still managed to escape to the United States, where he died the following February. His eldest son Joshua, who was 22, travelled to the States to bring his father's body back. The customs agents opened the coffin three times on his journey, convinced he was smuggling. But Joshua prevailed and his father was buried in St. John's Cemetery, York Mills, near their home. William Harrison's family were United Empire Loyalists who settled first in Nova Scotia, then on north Yonge St. William fought in the War of 1812 and was decorated for his bravery. He married Elizabeth Wright in 1813 and they had eleven children. In 1815 he bought the land where Harrison Rd. stands today, north of York Mills and east of Bayview. One of the provisions of William's will was that a house be built for his family on his property. In 1839 the house was built, and it was occupied by his descendants until 1943.

HAZELTON AVENUE

Avenue Rd./Bloor   There are three conflicting sources for this street name. Mike Filey in *Mount Pleasant Cemetery: An Illustrated Guide* suggested that it was named after a carriage driver named Joseph Hazelton (1823–1905), who lived at 7 Cumberland St. in the village of Yorkville and came to York from Ireland in 1850. In *Street Names* Mary Jarvis wrote that the name came from a man named George Hazelton White. John Ross Robertson, the earliest of these sources, wrote in *Landmarks of Canada* that it was named by a man who owned land in the area, George White, after his wife's family name, Hazelton. The truth may be that all these people were related, and maybe the last two were the same man, but until further evidence is unearthed, this serves as a good example of how difficult it can be to pinpoint the origin of street names.

HEATH STREET

Yonge/St. Clair

See **DEER PARK CRESCENT.**

HEINTZMAN STREET

Keele/Dundas   Theodore August Heintzman (1817–99), originally from Germany, came to America in 1850 and had a piano business in New York City and Buffalo. The American Civil War knocked the stuffing out of the piano business and he moved his family to Toronto. Heintzman first started making pianos in Toronto in the back room of his house on Duke St. (Adelaide) in 1860. Business was so successful that he soon moved it out into a factory on King St. In 1891 he moved the whole operation to a location in the Junction area (Keele/Dundas), where it remained for many years. The firm developed into a very successful operation, respected for its fine craftsmanship. Heintzman's started making grand pianos in 1886, and by the turn of the century had expanded into several other Canadian cities. During the last decade of his life, Heintzman lived in a grand Victorian mansion called the Birches, on Annette St., near his new factory. Heintzman & Co. manufactured player pianos until that fad died out in the 1920s. The company moved most of its production to Hanover, Ontario, in 1962. In 1978 it merged with the Sherlock-Manning Piano Co. The firm was sold again in 1981 to Sklar Manufacturing, who continued to make Heintzman pianos until 1986.

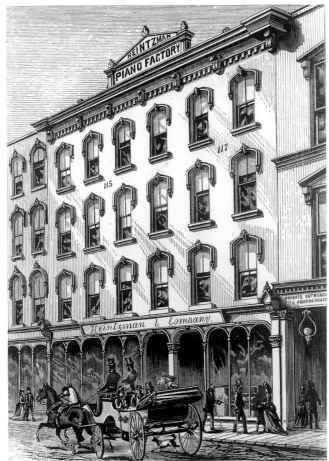

TRL T 30773

This wood engraving of the Heintzman factory on King just east of York appeared on their catalogue in 1874.

HENDRICK AVENUE

Oakwood/St. Clair   Hendrick Ave. lies right in the middle of a property that was once part of a market garden owned by Myles Hendrick and his wife Mary, who were originally from Ireland. Between 1877 and 1885 they bought two separate pieces of land, a total of 18 acres, above and below St. Clair. The orchards the Hendricks planted there were considered the best in the area, and they were large enough to employ as many as 50 fruit pickers at harvest time.

HENRY LANE TERRACE

Front/Jarvis   Henry Bowyer Joseph Lane, an English architect with family connections to the Boulton family, left his mark on several buildings still standing in Toronto. At the beginning of his career he lived in Toronto for six years (1841–47). During that time he designed Little Trinity Church (1843); part of Osgoode Hall (1844: the west wing, the porticoes, the loggia, and a central dome that was later taken down); the Church of St. George the Martyr (1844: burned down in 1955); the Church of the Holy Trinity (1846); and the second City Hall (1847) at the corner of Front and Jarvis. The centre of this last structure still exists in a reduced form as the

The central portion of Toronto's second City Hall (seen here in 1898) survives as part of the St. Lawrence Market.

St. Lawrence Market building. This street was named in the same competition in 1979 when Longboat Ave., Albert Frank Place, Douville Court, Portneuf Court and Scadding St. were named.

HEPBOURNE STREET

Bloor/Dovercourt
See **DOVERCOURT RD.**

HEYDON PARK ROAD

College/Dovercourt   Heydon Villa, a mansion made of red brick, stood just south of College St. and west of Dovercourt Rd., with lovely gardens stretching to the south. George Taylor Denison III (1839–1925) built his home in 1864, just after his marriage. He was the son of George Taylor Denison II (1816–73), and grew up on the neighbouring lot to the west at Rusholme. George named his new house after Headon, Yorkshire, which was the birthplace of his great-grandfather, John Denison (1755–1824), who had lived at Brookfield, the lot to the east. Colonel Denison was a lawyer and an officer in the militia, leading men during the Fenian Raids at Niagara in 1866 and again during the Northwest Rebellion in 1885. He was appointed a Police Magistrate in 1877, a position he held for 40 years. During the American Civil War, Colonel Denison got involved with Confederate agents and lost a good deal of money after buying back a captured ship from the Americans. He then gained some notoriety after winning a prize of 5,000 rubles from the Czar of Russia for an article he wrote on the history of cavalry. Heydon Villa, with 18-foot-high ceilings and a wide verandah lined with Doric columns, housed Colonel Denison's large library (2,000 books) and his extensive weapons collection. The widow's walk on the roof had an excellent view of downtown Toronto, and during the fire that burned much of downtown Toronto in 1904, the family gathered there to watch the spectacle. After Denison died in 1925, the grand old mansion stood empty for four years, and it was finally demolished in 1929. That's when Heydon Park Rd. was created. See **BELLEVUE AVE., BROOKFIELD ST., DENISON AVE., DOVERCOURT RD, RUSHOLME RD.**

HIGHLAND AVENUE

Mount Pleasant/St. Clair   The Scottish Ontario and Manitoba Land Company decided in 1907 to sell off its land in North Rosedale. The land was divided up and several new streets were created. The company's Canadian lawyers, Mowat, MacLennan and Co., were asked to find suitable names for the streets, and Roderick James MacLennan undertook the task. Highland Ave. lay along the ridge of a ravine, so MacLennan named it in honour of the company's Scottish shareholders. He named MacLennan Ave. not after himself, but after his former law professor, the Honourable Mr. Justice James MacLennan (1833–1915), who was an adviser to the land company and a Supreme Court judge. James MacLennan had a law practice in Toronto and Hamilton in partnership with Sir Oliver Mowat. Edgar Avenue was probably named by Roderick MacLennan too, after Sir James Edgar (1841–99), who had also been an adviser to the company. And MacLennan named Whitney Ave. after the Premier of Ontario at the time, Sir James Pliny Whitney (1843–1914). See **EDGAR AVE., MOWAT AVE., WHITNEY AVE.**

HIGH PARK AVENUE

Bloor/Keele
See **HOWARD PARK AVE.**

HOGARTH AVENUE

Broadview/Danforth   Thomas Hogarth was the principal of York Township School Section 10 in Riverside. In 1875 he bought a piece of land just east of Broadview and south of the Danforth and built a house there. In those days this area was dominated by orchards, market gardens and farms, with very few streets developed. Hogarth's daughter Elinor and her husband, Thomas Heys, a chemist and teacher, bought the house from him in 1882. They built an addition and lived there for many years. The street was named Hogarth in 1896, as the area began to be developed, and the house was given the number

58. The house passed out of the Heys family in 1964 and fell into a state of disrepair. In 1974 local citizens saved it from demolition and had it proclaimed a Heritage Property. Since then it has been lovingly restored by its various owners. The house has most of its original wood floors and large fireplaces. The small portion of land remaining with the house is now a pleasant garden with a good-sized vegetable patch and several tall old trees.

TRL 976-2-5

The Heys family relaxes on their lawn at 58 Hogarth Ave., circa 1900.

HOMEWOOD AVENUE

Carlton/Sherbourne   Home Wood was a house built in 1846–47 by George William Allan (1822–1901) near Sherbourne and Wellesley. His house was situated in the thickly forested northern section of his father's estate, Moss Park. George intended it to be a home for his new family and moved in with his bride, Louisa Robinson, just after it was completed. Sadly, she died just a few years later, in 1852. When his father died the next year, George inherited the Moss Park house and moved back there. Home Wood was eventually sold and ended up as the Wellesley Hospital, founded by Dr. Herbert Bruce. When the hospital needed to expand in 1964, the old building was finally torn down. George Allan was a prominent Toronto citizen, a lawyer and politician who at one point served as mayor (1855) and later as Speaker of the Senate (1888–91). He donated the five acres now bordered by Sherbourne, Gerrard, Jarvis and Carlton to the city for a public garden, which was opened by the Prince of Wales in 1860 and christened Allan Gardens. See **BRUCE PARK AVE.**

HOWARD PARK AVENUE
HOWARD STREET

TRL T 32140

John Howard, a talented architect, left High Park and Colborne Lodge to the city.

Dundas/Roncesvalles; Bloor/Sherbourne   John George Howard (1803–90) left far more to Toronto than two street names. His legacy, besides the many public and private buildings he designed as an architect, was High Park and Colborne Lodge. Howard, who had learned surveying and drafting in the British navy, immigrated to Canada with his wife Jemima in 1832, after surviving an exciting sea voyage that was nearly cut short by cholera, mutiny and shipwreck. Once safely in Upper Canada, Howard had the good fortune to hook up with Lieutenant Governor John Colborne, who hired him as a drawing teacher for Upper Canada College. In 1834 Howard was appointed City Surveyor, in which capacity he was responsible for the city's first plank sidewalks. Howard designed sewers, churches, jails and private homes. In 1838 he became City Engineer. His biggest project was the Provincial Lunatic Asylum on Queen Street (torn down in 1976). John Howard built his own house on his property just west of the city in 1836 and named it Colborne Lodge after his benefactor. He called his estate High Park because it stood on the highest bit of ground in the area. He and his wife decided in the 1870s to leave their house and 165-acre estate to the city of Toronto for a public park, with three conditions. The first was that Howard could live in his house until his death, with an income of $1,200 a year. The second was that alcoholic beverages would never be served in High Park. (This latter requirement resulted in High Park and the surrounding neighbourhoods being "dry" for nearly a century, with no liquor licences issued for restaurants.) A third condition was that the name of High Park never be changed. Another condition apparently demanded that no Roman Catholic ever be elected mayor. The city agreed, and John Howard became Forest Ranger of High Park; he made many improvements, including clearing land, building roads and drains, and designing gates and bridges. Howard designed the tomb where he and Jemima (who died in 1877) were buried, just southwest of Colborne Lodge. The iron railings around the tomb were from St. Paul's Cathedral in London, designed by Christopher Wren, and Howard bought them and had them shipped to Canada. In time the city added more land to the park and today it covers 400 acres. Colborne Lodge and the tomb still stand in the park, all three a tribute to a man who had the foresight to imagine how a beautiful park could enhance his city. See **COLBORNE ST., JARVIS ST., LAWTON BLVD., WOOD-LAWN AVE.**

HUBBARD BOULEVARD

Queen/Woodbine   Frederick Langdon Hubbard (1878–1953) was the son of William Peyton Hubbard (1842–1935), Toronto's first black alderman. This street was named after Frederick, the general manager of the Scarboro Beach Amusement Park, which for 18 years (1907–25) occupied the land between Leuty and MacLean south of Queen St. The boardwalk of the park ran along the beach right in the spot where Hubbard Blvd. is today. Modelled on the popular amusement park at Coney Island, the Scarboro Beach park offered a variety of amusements and recreation. Visitors to the park could ride the Scenic Railway (a rollercoaster that sped through painted tunnels), the Bump the Bumps (a huge slide with raised bumps), or they could Shoot the Chutes (a tall chute leading into a lagoon) in a small boat. When they grew tired of rides, they could go into the funhouses or the freak shows, or watch the daredevil acts: people jumped from the 125-foot tower into a net. Then they could go swimming, and after some refreshments, dance in the dance pavilions or just sit and listen to band concerts, with the night lit up around them with thousands of lights strung on the buildings. After the park closed in 1925 the area was laid out in a subdivision, with Hubbard Blvd. the only reminder of the glorious amusement park that once stood there.

A family enjoys their day out at Scarboro Beach Park, circa 1920.

HUMEWOOD DRIVE

St. Clair/Bathurst   William Hume Blake (1809–70) and his wife, Catherine Hume, named their country house Humewood, after their mutual grandfather's estate in county Wicklow, Ireland (they were first cousins). Their grandfather, whose name was also William Blake, had been a member of the British House of Commons who was murdered by Irish rebels in 1798. William and Catherine built their Humewood on the 25-acre property they bought in 1859, just northwest of today's St. Clair and Bathurst. The lane that led to their house eventually became today's Humewood Drive. Their son Edward (1833–1912), who became the second Premier of Ontario, called his house on Jarvis St.

Humewood too, and their grandson also called his home Humewood. The original Toronto Humewood, located at 40 Humewood Drive, burned down but was replaced with another house. This was bought by an Anglican charity in 1912 and converted into a home for unwed mothers called Humewood House, despite all the efforts of the Blake family to have the name changed. William Hume Blake had an impressive career as a lawyer and politician in Toronto. As a Reformer elected to the Legislative Assembly, he had the dubious privilege, along with his party leader, Robert Baldwin, of witnessing his effigy burnt in the street riots in 1849. The unrest occurred after he helped pass the Amnesty Bill that allowed William Lyon Mackenzie to return from exile. Blake's many appointments included Solicitor General (1848), Chancellor of the Court of Chancery (1849–62), Chancellor of the University of Toronto (1853), and a judge in the Court of Appeal (1864). See **ROBERT ST., WOODLAWN AVE.**

HURON STREET

Spadina/College   The Huron First Nations tribes were a confederacy made up of five tribes that lived in the Orillia/Midland area until 1649, when they were dispersed by their enemies, the Iroquois from upstate New York. "Huron" was a nickname meaning "ruffian" or "boar's head," given to them by the French fur traders because of the way the men wore their hair, sticking up in bristles. In their language their name was *Ouendat* (Wendat), meaning "people of the island." There were between 20,000 and 25,000 Huron before the French brought European diseases to Canada; only 9,000 remained when they were defeated by the Iroquois in 1649. The Hurons survived by growing vegetables and catching fish, living in longhouses in villages surrounded by palisades. Every 10 to 15 years they moved their villages to a new location, having depleted the soil and firewood supplies. The Iroquois waged a tireless campaign during the first half of the 17th century to get rid of the Hurons, who stood between them and the rich supplies of fur in central Ontario. The Hurons had made a military and trading alliance with the French in 1609 and by 1820 they dominated the fur trade in most of Ontario and part of Quebec. But by 1649 the Hurons were defeated and scattered. Some joined the Iroquois, some settled near Quebec City, and some moved west to Oklahoma.

INDIAN ROAD

Bloor/Parkside
See **SUNNYSIDE AVE.**

In 1913, Bloor St. east of Indian Rd. provided a wooden sidewalk for pedestrians and lots of mud for vehicles.

INKERMAN STREET

Bay/Bloor   In 1854 a decisive battle of the Crimean War was fought at Inkerman, a small village near Sebastopol on the Black Sea (now part of Ukraine), where the French and British troops defeated the Russians. The Crimean War was fought between Russia and the allied forces of France, Britain, Turkey and Sardinia. Many Canadians fought in the British Army, and Inkerman St. commemorates the once famous battle. See **RAGLAN AVE.**

JACKES AVENUE

Yonge/St. Clair   Joseph Jackes, a lawyer, lived with his wife and family in a house on the crest of Gallows Hill, as the Yonge/St. Clair hill was known in those days. Jackes, who was the son of Franklin Jackes, the first reeve of York Township, grew up at Castlefield, just north of Eglinton, and bought this house in 1865. Formerly the house had belonged to Walter Rose, who was married to Anna Ketchum (Jesse Ketchum's daughter). They had called the estate Rose Hill, but when Jackes moved in he changed the name to "The Elms," because of the lovely elm trees that surrounded the house. One of these trees had a huge horizontal limb, just perfect for hanging rebels from, and for years a rumour persisted that the tree had been used for a gallows during the Rebellion of 1837. The hill was known locally as Gallows Hill. Another rumour suggested that the name evolved after a mysterious hanged man was found there, but never identified. The nickname annoyed the family but it stuck. Joseph Jackes planted more fruit trees in the orchard and made improvements to the house. After his death in 1895, his son Edwin sold off some property south of the house and had Jackes Ave. laid out in about 1910. Gradually the city grew up around the house, and it was finally demolished in 1948. See **CASTLEFIELD AVE.**

JAMESON AVENUE

Queen/Lansdowne   Robert Sympson Jameson (1796–1854) held the positions of Attorney General of Upper Canada (1833–37) and then Vice Chancellor of the Court of Chancery (1837–50). Trained in England as a lawyer, he spent time in the West Indies as the Chief Justice of Dominica before his posting to Canada. Jameson was very unhappily married to Anna Brownell Jameson, a well-known writer. They spent most of their marriage apart, and even though he persuaded her to join him in Canada in 1836, she spent only a few months with him here before separating permanently from him and returning to England. She despised the provincial society she found in Toronto and wrote a travel book based on her time here: *Winter Studies and Summer Rambles in Canada*. Here is her thumbnail sketch of the city: "It is a little, ill-built town, on low land, at the bottom of a frozen bay, with one very ugly church, without tower or steeple, some government offices, built of staring red brick, in the most tasteless, vulgar style imaginable, three feet of snow all around, and the grey sullen, uninviting lake and the dark gloom of the pine forest bounding the prospect." (Robertson, 494) Despite his personal unhappiness, Jameson fulfilled his duties with diligence and participated in various social and official organizations in Toronto, including the Law Society, the Legislative Council, King's College, Trinity College, the Toronto Literary Club and the Toronto Society of Arts. In the late 1840s Jameson bought some land south of Queen in the area where Jameson Ave. runs today.

JARVIS STREET

Queen's Quay to Bloor between Sherbourne and Yonge   The Jarvis family owned the land in this area. William Jarvis was the Provincial Secretary and Registrar of Records from 1792 until his death in 1817. He passed on a huge debt load to his son, Samuel Peters Jarvis (1792–1857), who also took over his father's job as Secretary. William died while his son was in prison

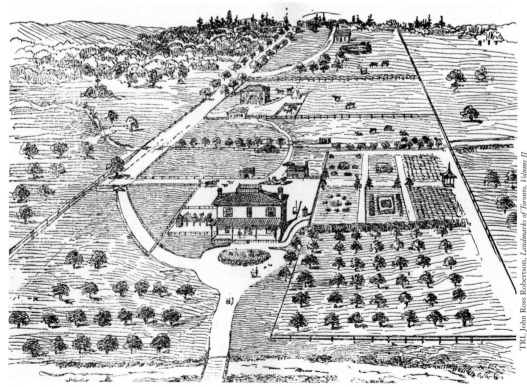

Samuel Jarvis's Hazel Burn sat in the middle of today's Jarvis St., just north of Queen.

charged with murder. Samuel, then 25, had fought a duel with 18-year-old John Ridout, as a result of bad feeling between their families and a number of angry exchanges between the two young men. Ridout anticipated and fired on the count of two. He missed, and then Samuel fired on the count of three and killed him. Although he was arrested and jailed, Samuel was later acquitted. In 1824 he built a house on the property, about where Shuter and Jarvis intersect today, and called it Hazel Burn. He held the office of Chief Superintendent of the Department of Indian Affairs between 1837 and 1845, but then he was dismissed because of poor management. His accumulated debts drove him to sell off part of his land. Between 1846 and 1851 John Howard supervised the subdivision, creating Jarvis, Mutual and George (north of Shuter) streets. Hazel Burn was partially demolished because it stood right smack in the centre of the proposed Jarvis St. Mutual had been a country road that marked the mutual boundary between Hazel Burn and John McGill's property. Howard laid out Jarvis St. as a wide, tree-lined boulevard and by the 1870s it was the most fashionable address in Toronto, with stately rows of mansions along each side of the street. See **McGILL ST., HOWARD PARK AVE., LAWTON BLVD.**

In the 1890s Jarvis St. was a wide boulevard lined with the houses of rich and prestigious Torontonians.

JOHN STREET

King/Spadina
See **SIMCOE ST.**

JORDAN STREET

King/Yonge   Jordan Post (1767–1845) was the first watchmaker and clock-maker in the town of York. He came from Connecticut with his family in 1802 and bought the land between Yonge and Bay along King St. He set up a store and operated a successful watchmaking business. He ventured into real estate and made a great profit buying and selling properties. Post also served on the town council and donated money for the establishment of a common school in York and for a Presbyterian church. In his '60s he moved to some land he owned in Scarborough and began a lumber business. Melinda St. was named after his wife, Melinda Woodruff.

KEELE STREET

Bloor to Steeles between Jane and Dufferin   William Keele, a lawyer, lived in a farmhouse he called Glenside just south of today's Dundas and Keele. He bought the 100-acre property in 1834. Keele bought more land in 1840 and in 1857 created Carleton Race Course. Here in 1860 the Queen's Plate was run for the first time. His son Charles sold the racetrack in 1882 and after his death in 1884 the whole property was sold. The CPR terminal was opened in 1884 and the surrounding area (known as the Junction) began to be developed, with streets laid out and houses built.

KELSO AVENUE

Avenue Rd./Wilson   John Joseph Kelso (1864–1935), who worked as a reporter for two Toronto newspapers (the *World* and the *Globe*) in the 1880s, became known as one of the most influential social reformers of the late 19th and early 20th centuries. He founded the Toronto Humane Society (originally for the prevention of cruelty to animals and children) in 1887, the Fresh Air Fund and the Santa Claus Fund (to help the poor go on trips out of the city) in 1888, and the Children's Aid Society in 1891. From 1893 until 1934 he served as the Superintendent of Neglected Children in Ontario, overseeing the establishment of children's aid societies in the province. Known as "the children's friend," he worked tirelessly to improve the condition of underprivileged children, supporting the creation of playgrounds, mother's allowance, special juvenile courts, legalized adoption and the closing of children's reformatories.

KEW BEACH CRESCENT
KEW BEACH AVENUE

Woodbine/Queen   The original Kew Gardens (also known as the Royal Botanic Gardens) are located in Richmond upon Thames, Greater London, England. The Princess Augusta, who was King George III's mother, founded Kew Gardens in 1759. The botanic gardens, which now cover 288 acres, are a centre for scientific research and conservation, with millions of plant specimens from around the world. The Canadian Kew Gardens were created by a couple from England, Joseph and Jane Williams. In 1853 they bought some property near Queen and Woodbine and built a cabin there, naming their farm Kew Farms after the area in London. By 1879 they had acquired more land and opened the Canadian Kew Gardens, a park that offered various activities: camping, dancing, refreshments, puppet shows and band music. People came to picnic or stay in small cottages, and on holidays there were special entertainments like baseball and bonfires. The Williams named their youngest son Kew, and the house he built in 1902 still stands at the edge of the park at 30 Lee Avenue. For years it was the official residence of the parkkeeper. In 1907 the city bought the park from the Williams family for use as a public park, clearing away the cottages and adding tennis courts, wooden bobsled runs in the winter, a bathing pavilion, a bandshell, lawn bowling and other improvements. After the city bought the Scarboro Beach Amusement Park in 1925, they began to develop a larger park that spread right across all the eastern beaches from Woodbine to Nursewood Rd. It opened on Victoria Day, 1932, with a 4,800-foot boardwalk, a public boathouse, a lavatory and an athletic field. Although the Parks Commissioner at the time wanted to call the new park Kew Beach Park, the residents of Balmy Beach to the east strongly objected, and it was called the Eastern Beaches Park. Kew Gardens remains a popular and attractive city park, the site of many public events, including a jazz festival every July and a craft show every June. See **HUBBARD BLVD.**

Looking east along King St. from Yonge in 1835, with (from left) the jail, court house and the third St. James Church.

KING STREET

Don Valley to Roncesvalles between Queen and Front One of the earliest streets to be laid out in the town of York, King St. was named for King George III (b. 1738, r. 1760–1820), who was the reigning monarch at the time. Although he was known as "mad King George," today his symptoms have been diagnosed as possible signs of porphyria, a disease that can poison the nervous system and the brain. Between November 1788 and April 1789 he suffered his first attack of wild behaviour, but then was able to live a fairly normal life until 1810, when the disease (or madness) hit him in full force and incapacitated him until his death in 1820. Despite his illness, King George apparently held the love and respect of his subjects throughout a difficult reign marked by strife: England lost the American colonies after the American Revolution and fought against France in the Napoleonic Wars.

Gallagher's delivery truck, the first in Toronto, on the south side of King St. east of Church in 1907.

KIPLING AVENUE

Lake Shore Blvd. to Steeles between Islington and Martin Grove   There is no proof that this street was named after Rudyard Kipling (1865–1936), the writer who left us *The Jungle Book* (1894), *Kim* (1901), *The Just So Stories* (1902) and *Puck of Pook's Hill* (1906), as well as many other novels and poetry. But a popular legend holds that the street was named after Kipling when he visited Toronto in 1907 while he was touring North America. He was scheduled to open the Woodbridge Fair, but cancelled at the last minute, and somehow the road that led to Woodbridge became known as Kipling Ave.

LAIRD DRIVE

Bayview/Eglinton   Laird Drive was named after Leaside was laid out as a railway town by the Canadian Northern Railway, just before the First World War. It was named after Prime Minister Robert Laird Borden (1854–1937), who led the country from 1911 to 1920. Laird was his mother's maiden name. Born in Nova Scotia, Borden was a self-made man: he started as a teacher and then, after qualifying as a lawyer in 1878, he quickly rose to the head of a law firm in Halifax by 1890. In 1896 he was first elected to Parliament and by 1901 he was the leader of the Liberal-Conservative Party. Opposition to the Laurier government's Reciprocity Agreement with the United States formed his platform in the election of 1911. He used his considerable political skill to form alliances with anti-Laurier factions to defeat the government. During the war he proved to be a strong national leader, introducing the Emergency War Measures Act (1914), direct taxation (1916 and 1917), the nationalization of the railway, and conscription. This last controversial measure resulted in the formation of a Union government led by Borden, which was a coalition between Liberals and Conservatives who favoured compulsory military service. The coalition won the election in 1917. Borden believed Canada proved itself as a nation by its impressive performance in the First World War. After the war he was an outspoken champion of the autonomy of Canada and other British dominions, and his work at the Paris Peace Conference in 1919 contributed to the transformation of the British Empire to the British Commonwealth of Nations. After he retired from politics in 1920, Borden served as chancellor of Queen's University in Kingston from 1924 to 1930. See **HANNA RD., LEA AVE.**

LANGTON AVENUE

Mount Pleasant/Lawrence   This street was named in 1913 after the Langtons, a distinguished family in Canada in the 19th and 20th centuries. One was Auditor General of Canada, one was an architect, two wrote books about life in early Upper Canada, and one was the librarian of University College and an influential editor. John Langton (1808–1904) settled in the Fenelon Falls area of Upper Canada, near Peterborough, in 1833. He represented that area in the Legislative Assembly from 1851 to 1855, and was Auditor General from 1855 to 1878. As vice chancellor of the University of Toronto, Langton was a key figure in the planning and building of University College between 1856 and 1859. He had to negotiate between the Governor General, Sir Edmund Head; the architects, Frederic Cumberland and William George Storm; and the principal of the university, Dr. John McCaul. Langton wrote his brother in England very amusing accounts of his struggles to bring the building to completion. In *No Mean City* Eric Arthur relates the process in some detail. At one point the plans hung in balance because the Governor General (apparently a vain and autocratic master) wanted it to face east rather than south (the entire layout had been designed for a southern exposure) and was only dissuaded because of his concern that a handsome elm tree would have to be sacrificed for an eastern exposure: " … but you Canadians are prejudiced against trees," Head commented (Langton, 284). At an earlier point in the plans, when Cumberland was proposing a Gothic style, Head disagreed and "recommended Italian, showing us an example of the style, a palazzo at Siena, which if he were not governor-general and had written a book on art, I should have called one of the ugliest buildings I ever saw." (Langton, 292) These letters were later edited by John's son, William Alexander Langton (1854-1933) and published in book form in 1926 as *Early Days in Upper Canada: Letters of John Langton from the Backwoods of Upper Canada*. William was the architect in the family, noted for his design of the Toronto Golf Club in Mississauga in 1913. His brother Hugh Hornby Langton (1862–1953) became the registrar at the University of Toronto in 1887 and the chief librarian in 1892. He was responsible for the establishment of the library system that is the foundation of the university's libraries today. He was also an influential editor at the university and the founder of the *Canadian Historical Review*. In 1950 he published an edition of the work of the other writer in the family, his aunt Anne Langton, whose journals were collected as *A Gentlewoman in Upper Canada: The Journals of Anne Langton*. A talented artist who had a genteel upbringing, Anne came with her parents and brother John to live in the wilds of Fenelon Falls in 1833. Undaunted by the dramatic change in her life, Anne learned what she needed to survive in her new country: soap and candle making, butchery, how to glaze windows and sew upholstery. She was consulted on medical matters by her neighbours and filled in as parson when John was away on business (John himself was not ordained but acted as parson because there was no one else to do it). Anne sketched and painted and wrote in her journals, but also established a library and a school in the area. Her journals provide a fascinating and practical description of pioneer life in Upper Canada, with telling details about a pioneer woman's backbreaking daily routine. See **McCAUL ST.**

University College was completed in 1859, facing south instead of east to save an old elm tree.

LANSDOWNE AVENUE

Queen to St. Clair between Dufferin and Roncesvalles   Lansdowne Ave. was named in 1883 by the village council of Parkdale, in honour of the new Governor General of Canada: Henry Charles Keith Petty-Fitzmaurice, the 5th Marquis of Lansdowne (1845–1927). Lansdowne performed his duties admirably from 1883 to 1888, during a tumultuous period in Canadian history. The Northwest Rebellion broke out and the Canadian Pacific Railway was completed, despite the scandals that rocked the country. His distinguished political career also included Lord of the Treasury (1869–72) and Under-Secretary for War (1872–74) in England, and Viceroy of India (1888–93).

LAURIER AVENUE

Parliament/Wellesley   Sir Wilfrid Laurier (1841–1919), Prime Minister of Canada from 1896 to 1911, is remembered for his charisma and his skill at finding compromise. He began as a lawyer, then became a journalist, and first came to Ottawa as a Liberal MP in 1871. His deeply felt desire to heal the division between the battling English and French in Canada was fuelled by the execution of Louis Riel after the Northwest Rebellion in 1885, and governed many of his decisions throughout his political life. In 1887 he took over the leadership of the Liberal party, and after establishing a solid support base in Quebec, won the federal election in 1896 and became Prime Minister. During his tenure he undertook the construction of a second railway system, which was popular with the electorate, but proved to be very costly for the nation in the years to come. He was instrumental in the birth of two new provinces – Alberta and Saskatchewan – and he helped to consolidate Canada as a nation during a time of increased industrialization and growing population. His efforts to reach a compromise on the separate school system alienated many of his French-Canadian supporters, who believed he had betrayed their interests, and his support for reciprocity (free trade) with the United States ultimately defeated him in the election of 1911. As the leader of the Opposition during the First World War, Laurier vigorously opposed conscription, an issue that divided the country. The French were against conscription and the English were for it, and in 1917 some of his own party who disagreed with his stand on voluntary enlistment crossed the floor to join Robert Borden's Unionist Party. The man who had worked for so many years to unite his country now symbolized the deep divisions between French and English, and he was defeated in the 1917 election. He was determined to reunite his party and keep fighting for Canadian unity, but he died in 1919 just as that battle was beginning. See **LAIRD AVE.**

LAWRENCE AVENUE

Port Union to Royal York between Eglinton and Wilson/York Mills   At the turn of the 19th century, Lawrence Ave. consisted of a grassy stretch of road allowance between the Lawrence properties at Yonge and their holdings in the Don Valley. The family came from Yorkshire and settled in the area in 1829. They bought a property on the northeast side of Yonge and Lawrence and farmed the land. Later they created market gardens, tanneries, opened a general store and built a sawmill in the Don Valley near Bayview and Lawrence. Peter Lawrence bought the original farmland in 1829; by 1836 he held the position of Justice of the Peace for the village of Eglinton. Jacob Lawrence, who at one point ran a tannery on the southwest corner of Lawrence and Yonge, built a sawmill in the Don Valley just east of Bayview in 1845. Another member of the family, George Lawrence, ran a general store on Yonge north of Lawrence, which included a post office and a feed mill. The Lawrence farm was sold in 1907 to the company led by Wilfred Servington Dinnick, who was developing the area. Dinnick named his garden suburb Lawrence Park, after the family who had lived and worked in the area for nearly 70 years. See **DINNICK CRESCENT.**

LAWTON BOULEVARD

Yonge/St. Clair   Lawton Park was a house built by the architect John Howard (he took over from Henry Bowyer Lane), originally under the direction of Colonel Arthur Carthew, who bought six acres of the Deer Park estate in

1847. He called his estate Lawton Park and planned to live in his new house when he got married. However, his fiancée suffered a mysterious and fatal accident at the entrance to the grounds when she was on her way to inspect the building, and the broken-hearted Carthew sold the partially completed house to John Fisken in 1848. Howard completed the construction, salvaging the black walnut trim from Hazel Burn, the Jarvis house that was demolished around the same time. Fisken, a businessman and the founder of the Imperial Bank, kept the name Lawton Park, and his family lived there for many years. The house stood at the corner of Heath St. West and Yonge, with a great sweeping circular drive, an English landscaped garden, greenhouses and a dove house. It passed to other owners in 1904, who renamed it Huntley Lodge, and it was demolished in 1935. Lawton Blvd. used to be called Old Yonge St., where Yonge St. swerved to bypass a ravine. After the newer part of the street was built through the ravine, many people still preferred the old route to avoid walking through the hollow by the Mount Pleasant Cemetery. See **DEER PARK CRESCENT, JARVIS ST.**

The first owner of Lawton Park sold it because of his fiancée's tragic death on the grounds. Circa 1896.

LEA AVENUE
LEACREST ROAD
LEADALE AVENUE

Bayview/Moore   The family that left its name in Leaside first came to Upper Canada in 1818 from Lancashire, England, via the United States (which they did not care for). John Lea bought a 200-acre property between Bayview and the Don River. Here he lived in a log cabin and established a dairy farm and an orchard. By 1829 he was prosperous enough to build a brick house with four chimneys (since any chimneys built after the first were taxed, four were considered a luxury). He called his house Leaside. It stood where Lea Ave. is today. When he died in 1851 he left his house and property to his two sons, John and William. William bought an adjoining property in 1854 and built an eight-sided house. Octagonal houses were a fad at that time in the United States and Canada. There he farmed and brought up his family. He was a justice of the peace and served on the first Council for York Township in 1850. In the early years of the 20th century, the Canadian Northern Railway planned the town of Leaside, intending to develop the community as a railway town with all the facilities to service the railway: railway yards, machine shops and homes for the railway workers. Before the onset of the First World War in 1914, the railway company spent two million dollars on their model community. The war put a stop to their immediate plans, but industries moved during the war and gradually the area developed. See **LAIRD DR., HANNA RD.**

LEACOCK CRESCENT

Leslie/York Mills   Between 1915 and 1925, Stephen Leacock (1869–1944) was the most famous humorist in the world. Many of his books were compilations of his magazine articles, which were prolific. In *Sunshine Sketches of a Little Town* he described the fictional town of Mariposa, using his trademark combination of caustic wit and affection to poke fun at the respectable Canadians who dwelt there. Leacock's worldview politics were turn-of-the-century conservative: he opposed excessive materialism and the worship of technology. He came to Canada at the age of seven and attended Upper Canada College, where he taught for nine years after graduating. In 1903 he received his Ph.D. in economics and political science and went on to teach at McGill University in Montreal, where he remained until he retired to his home in Orillia (the prototype for Mariposa), about 75 miles due north of Toronto, in 1936. He won many honours during his life (including the Governor General's Award in 1937 and the Lorne Pierce Medal) and three years after he died, the Stephen Leacock Memorial Medal was established. This is awarded each year to the best humorous book published by a Canadian. Here is a sampling of the winners over the years: Earle Birney's *Turvey* (1950), Robertson Davies' *Leaven of Malice* (1955), Farley Mowat's *The Boat Who Wouldn't Float* (1970), W.P. Kinsella's *The Fencepost Chronicles* (1987), and Joseph Kertes' *Winter Tulips* (1989).

LEADER LANE

Yonge/King
See **GLENGROVE AVE.**

Looking north on Leader Lane in 1875 to King St. E.

LEE AVENUE

Queen/Woodbine   Kew Street until 1883, Lee Ave. was named after a man who owned a large property in the area, with gardens stretching from Queen

St. to the water. Walter Sutherland Lee (1837–1902) was the director of the Western Canada Loan and Savings Company and held many civic appointments. He served as the president of the Mechanics Institute (the forerunner of the public library), and chairman of the Toronto General Hospital. Leuty St. was named after his wife, Emma Mary Leuty. See **KEW BEACH CRESCENT, HUBBARD BLVD.**

LESLIE STREET

Lake Ontario to Ivy between Coxwell and Pape; Eglinton to Steeles between Don Mills Rd. and Bayview George Leslie came to Toronto from Scotland in 1824 and found work as a gardener and a builder (he worked on the construction of the Parliament Buildings and Upper Canada College). In 1837 he opened the first seed store in Upper Canada. In 1845 he moved east of the Don River and began to buy land. Eventually he accumulated 200 acres and ran a prosperous nursery business there. Leslie was elected to the Toronto City Council in 1862. In 1860 Leslieville became an official address, with the post office at the corner of today's Queen and Curzon streets. George Leslie was postmaster until Leslieville was annexed to Toronto in 1884.

LIPPINCOTT STREET

Bathurst/College Captain Richard Lippincott came to New Brunswick originally from New Jersey, where he fought in a band of pro-British guerrillas in the American Revolution. He was tried in connection with the hanging of one of the rebels (an act of revenge after his brother-in-law was brutally murdered by the opposing faction), and he remained in protective custody during the rest of the war. In 1793 he came to York as a staunch loyalist and was granted 3,000 acres in the Richmond Hill area. His daughter, Esther Borden Lippincott, married George Taylor Denison (1783–1853), who built Belle Vue near Spadina and College. The money and land she brought with her to the marriage established George Denison's fortune. Richard lived with his daughter and son-in-law at Belle Vue until his death in 1826. See **BELLEVUE AVE., DENISON AVE.**

LISGAR STREET

Queen/Dovercourt   Sir John Young, Baron of Lisgar (1807–76), was Governor General of Canada from 1869 to 1872. Before his appointment to Canada he had held several important positions in the British government: Lord of the Treasury, Chief Secretary for Ireland and colonial appointments in the Ionian Islands and Australia. In Canada, he was much admired by Sir John A. Macdonald. Lisgar supported Confederation and tried to ease the tensions between Canada and the United States.

LITTLE NORWAY CRESCENT

Bathurst/Lake Shore Blvd.   Little Norway was the name given to the area south of Lake Shore Blvd. just opposite Toronto Island Airport during the Second World War. Norway had been invaded in the spring of 1940 and the Norwegian forces evacuated to Britain. After negotiations with the Canadian government, the Norwegian Air Force relocated to Canada in the summer of 1940 for further training. All the Canadian airfields were being used, so the little airport on Toronto Island, which had just been built a year and a half earlier, was pressed into duty. The pilots and their crews were given the plot of land just across the channel to build their accommodations and training school. The area soon became known as Little Norway. They crossed the channel to the airport on a small ferry pulled by a wire rope. By 1941 there were 1,000 Norwegians crowded together at the base, and it relocated to a site near Gravenhurst. Then the RCAF used the facilities at Little Norway until the end of the war.

Norwegian Air Force trainees disembark from the ferry, with Little Norway in the background, 1940.

LLOYD GEORGE AVENUE

Brown's Line/Lake Shore Blvd.   David Lloyd George (1863–1945), 1st Earl of Dwyfor, led Britain as Prime Minister during the First World War. He headed a coalition government of Liberals and Conservatives from 1916 to 1922, when he resigned. The son of a Welsh headmaster, he trained as a solicitor and won a seat in Parliament in 1890 as a fervent Welsh nationalist and Radical. As such he opposed England's participation in the Boer War. He was appointed president of the Board of Trade in 1905 and Chancellor of the Exchequer in 1908, laid the foundations of the welfare state with his National Insurance Bill of 1911 and an Unemployment Insurance Bill soon after that. During the chaos and pressures of the First World War, Lloyd George's loss of confidence in Prime Minister Herbert Henry Asquith led to Asquith's resignation, and the king asked Lloyd George to lead the government in late 1916. He worked hard to unite the Allies in their struggle against Germany, and his efforts proved instrumental in bringing the United States into the war. After the Allied victory was declared in 1918, Lloyd George helped to negotiate the Treaty of Versailles between Germany and the Allies. The next few years were difficult for Britain and Lloyd George, with labour unrest, civil war in Ireland and financial woes brought on by the long war. All these troubles weakened his support, and in 1922 he resigned. Lloyd George had a colourful, magnetic personality with a genius for politics and a formidable wit. His less attractive qualities were his love of secrecy and a lack of scrupulousness in regard to honours and appointments, which led to several scandals during his political career. He left an indelible mark on the political scene in Britain in the 20th century.

LONGBOAT AVENUE

Parliament/Front   Thomas Charles Longboat (1887–1949), known as the Bronze Mercury, was a champion long-distance runner who won the Boston Marathon in 1907, the Toronto Ward's Marathon three years in a row (1906–8) and the World's Professional Marathon Championship in 1909. He was born on the Six Nations Reserve near Brantford, Ontario. During the 1908 London Olympics Marathon, he collapsed, probably from a drug overdose, and a controversy ensued. Longboat had many disagreements with his managers because he insisted on using his own training methods, which proved successful: in 1912 he set a record for running 15 miles at 1:18:10. During the First World War he served as a dispatch runner with the 180th Sportsmen's Battalion. When he returned home he found that his wife Lauretta had remarried after being informed that he had been killed. He remarried and had four children. He worked as a street cleaner in Toronto until he retired to the Six Nations Reserve in 1944. This street was named in a public competition held in 1979 to designate new streets in the St. Lawrence Neighbourhood housing development. See **ALBERT FRANCK PLACE, DOUVILLE COURT, HENRY LANE TERRACE, PORTNEUF COURT, SCADDING ST.**

LOUNT STREET

Greenwood/Gerrard   Samuel Lount (1791–1838) was one of the two Rebels who were hanged for their participation in the Rebellion of 1837. The other was Peter Matthews. They were sentenced to hang by Chief Justice John Beverley Robinson, and despite a petition signed by 5,000 people, they were executed on April 12, 1838. Lount's final words were, "I'm not ashamed of anything I've done. I trust in God and I'll die like a man." He had to comfort his friend Sheriff William Jarvis, whose duty it was to carry out the sentence. Samuel Lount was a blacksmith and lived in Holland Landing. He was elected to the Assembly in 1834, then defeated in the election of 1836, when the government was accused of corrupt election practices. A staunch Mackenzie supporter, he led a group of men down Yonge St. in the December 1837 Rebellion. They were turned back at College St. after a few shots were exchanged. Two days later 1,000 Loyalists marched on Montgomery's Tavern with their cannon and muskets and confronted the rebels, a group of between 300 and 400 men armed with pitchforks and farm implements. It was all over very quickly. The rebels were rounded up and marched down Yonge St., tied together with ropes. Some died in prison; many were exiled and two of the ringleaders, Peter Matthews and Samuel Lount, were publicly hanged. See **BEVERLEY ST., ROSEDALE HEIGHTS DR.**

MACDONELL AVENUE

Queen/Lansdowne   The Macdonells were a prominent Loyalist family who settled in Canada at the time of the American Revolution. Originally from Scotland, they lived in New York State until the war broke out and they were forced to flee north to Canada. Alex Macdonnell (1762–1842) had fought with Butler's Rangers during the war. In 1798 he was granted lot 32, which ran from Queen St. to Bloor in the area where Macdonell Ave. now runs. He lived in a house he had built in the city at the corner of Adelaide and John. Macdonell held the position of Sheriff of the Home District from 1792 to

1805 and served in the Assembly from 1800 to 1812 and from 1820 to 1823. His brother Angus Macdonell, who also sat in the Assembly, was drowned along with 39 others in a storm aboard the schooner *Speedy* in 1804. It was a descendant of this family, James George Macdonell, who inherited the land in Parkdale and built a house near Macdonell and Queen St. In the 1870s the village of Parkdale began to be developed and Macdonell Ave. was laid out. James Macdonell planted trees along each side of the new street.

MACLENNAN AVENUE

Mount Pleasant/St. Clair
See **HIGHLAND AVE.**

MACPHERSON AVENUE

Avenue Rd./Davenport
See **CHESTNUT PARK.**

MAITLAND PLACE
MAITLAND STREET

Jarvis/Wellesley   Sir Peregrine Maitland (1777–1854) was Lieutenant Governor of Upper Canada from 1818 to 1828, and Lieutenant Governor of Nova Scotia from 1828 to 1834. He began his career at the age of 15, when he joined the British Army. By 1814 he was a Major General and in 1815 led a brigade at the Battle of Waterloo, after which he was knighted. His term as Lieutenant Governor in York was marked by growing dissension and polarization between the established Family Compact and the Reformers. He took a very rigid, conservative stand against the Reformers, and his intractability contributed to the dissatisfaction that led to the Rebellion of 1837. Maitland had no love for the town of York (many people at the time considered the site unhealthy); he built himself a summer home near Niagara and recommended changing the capital to Kingston. Maitland's tenure in Nova Scotia was much less controversial than the time he spent in York. He went on to head the

British Army at Madras and then to the Cape of Good Hope as Governor in 1844. He was generally considered ineffective by this time, and retired in 1847. See **RICHMOND ST.**

MANNING AVENUE

College/Bathurst   Alexander Manning (1819–1903) came from Ireland to Upper Canada in 1834 and began his career as an apprentice to a carpenter. He made his fortune as a builder and contractor and later on as a real estate developer. The Parliamentary Library in Ottawa and Egerton Ryerson's Normal School in Toronto, the Welland Canal, and the railways were all projects he was involved in. In 1856 he entered politics as an alderman on the Toronto City Council. After a second term he ran for mayor in 1873 and won. He won again in 1885. Manning bought some land west of Bathurst and south of Bloor St. for development and built many houses there. In 1888 Manning Ave. was named after him (it had formerly been called Hope St.). See **RYERSON AVE.**

MARION STREET

Queen/Roncesvalles
See **O'HARA AVE.**

MARLBOROUGH AVENUE

Avenue Rd./Dupont   John Churchill, the Duke of Marlborough (1650–1722), was one of the most famous English generals. His military skill and attention to detail contributed to his many victories. After the revolution in 1688, in which Marlborough switched his allegiance at the last moment from King James II to William of Orange, he was made the Earl of Marlborough. His marriage to Sarah Jennings, attendant to Princess Anne (who was later to become Queen), played a key role in his political fortunes. In 1702 the War of the Spanish Succession was declared. England, the Netherlands and Austria united to fight France, and Marlborough led their combined forces. For the next several years Marlborough carried out brilliant campaigns against the

French troops, and was showered with honours. Blenheim Palace was built for him at public expense. Intrigues at court resulted in Marlborough's fall from royal favour, and in 1712 he left the country for the Continent, where he remained until Queen Anne's death in 1714. He was buried in Westminster Abbey. Winston Churchill, Prime Minister of Britain during the Second World War, was one of his descendants.

MASSEY STREET

King/Strachan   The Massey-Ferguson farm machinery factory stood on King St. West opposite Massey St. for many years. The company was established by Daniel Massey (1798–1856) in Newcastle in the 1840s. His son, Hart Almerrin Massey (1823–96), developed the company into the largest manufacturer of farm machinery in the world, joining with its chief competitor to

The Massey-Harris Co. on King St. W. in 1926.

form the Massey-Harris Co. Ltd. in 1891. The Masseys were devout Methodists and great benefactors to Toronto. Two of Hart's sons, Charles Albert and Frederic Victor, died prematurely and Hart built Massey Hall and the Fred Victor Mission in their memories. His other son, Chester, devoted himself to running the Massey Foundation, a philanthropic organization responsible for, among other projects, the creation of Hart House and Massey College, both at the University of Toronto. Chester's two sons, Charles Vincent (1887–1967) and Raymond Hart (1896–1983) both achieved fame in very different pursuits. Vincent Massey was appointed Governor General in 1952, the first person born in Canada to hold that position. Raymond Massey was a successful actor famous for his film portrayal of Abraham Lincoln, and as Dr. Gillespie on the television series *Dr. Kildare*.

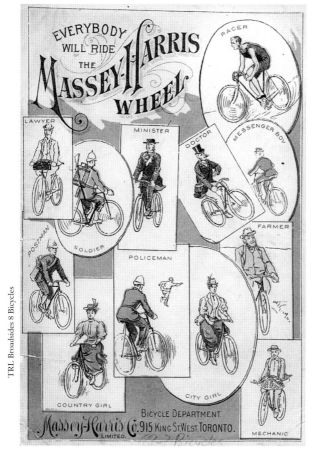

TRL Broadsides 8 Bicycles

Massey-Harris manufactured bicycles in the 1890s to meet the growing demand from consumers.

McCAUL STREET

Queen/University   John McCaul was ordained in Ireland in 1833 and came to Toronto in 1838 to be the principal of Upper Canada College. From there he took up the position of vice-president and professor of classics at King's College in 1842. When John Strachan resigned as principal in 1848, McCaul took over, staying on as president when the college was renamed University College in 1853. While he was principal, the impressive new building was built, between 1856 and 1859. McCaul remained principal until he retired in 1880. He had a great interest in music and organized concerts and musical societies. See **LANGTON AVE., TRINITY CIRCLE.**

McGILL STREET

Yonge/Carlton
See **CARLTON ST.**

McMASTER AVENUE

Avenue Rd./Dupont   William McMaster (1811–87) is chiefly remembered as the benefactor of McMaster University in Hamilton. He came to Upper Canada from Ireland in 1833 and worked as a clerk in a dry goods store. In recognition of his hard work he was made a partner, and after 10 years he took over the business and built it up to the point where he could hand it over to his nephews and devote his time to financial matters. He founded the Canadian Bank of Commerce and served as its president for 15 years. In 1867, after a brief stint as a Liberal Member of Parliament, McMaster was appointed to the Senate. A devout Baptist, McMaster helped to establish the first Baptist congregation in Toronto in 1840, and in 1874 he generously gave $60,000 to the building fund of the Jarvis Street Baptist Church. He founded the Toronto

Baptist College in 1881, and left a legacy of nearly one million dollars to establish a Baptist university when he died in 1887. McMaster University was formed in 1888, the result of a union between the Toronto Baptist College and Woodstock College. The fledgling university was located on Bloor St. just west of the Royal Ontario Museum. It relocated to Hamilton in 1930. The McMasters lived in a mansion east of Yonge St. on the north side of Bloor, and they built a summer home called Rathnelly (after McMaster's birthplace in Ireland) on their country property west of Avenue Rd. and north of Dupont, remembered in today's Rathnelly Ave. Poplar Plains Rd. was a rough country lane that wound through their land up the hill to St. Clair. The tablelands north of Davenport had been called the poplar plains for some time before the McMasters bought their property in the early 1850s.

MELBOURNE AVENUE

Queen/Dufferin   William Lamb, Lord Melbourne (1779–1848), was Prime Minister of England when Victoria came to the throne in 1837. He became her chief adviser and the young monarch relied on him to guide her in the early years of her reign. Melbourne was an old-fashioned Conservative with no interest in parliamentary reform or the difficulties of the poor. His favourite response to any proposals for change was, "Why not leave it alone?" Melbourne advised Queen Victoria not to read Dickens because he wrote about the lower classes, which Melbourne considered an unsuitable subject for the Queen to be concerned about. After Victoria's marriage to Prince Albert in 1840 and the defeat of the Conservatives in 1841, Melbourne's influence on Victoria waned. See **QUEEN ST.**

MELINDA STREET

Yonge/King
See **JORDAN ST.**

MERCER STREET

King/Spadina   Andrew Mercer (1778–1871) died rich without a will. The government used most of his estate to build the Mercer Reformatory on King St. east of Dufferin. The Reformatory (a gloomy Victorian edifice) was an institution for reforming "fallen women" that was used from 1880 until 1969, when it was demolished. The use to which Mercer's fortune was put is somewhat ironic. At the end of his life Mercer lived with a bad-tempered housekeeper and her son. When he died, the housekeeper claimed that her son was Mercer's illegitimate heir, producing a will and a marriage certificate. These were declared forgeries by the court. Mercer had come to York in 1801 and held the position of a junior clerk for the Executive Council and was paymaster for the militia during the war of 1812. He operated a store and later a mortgage and loan business. Then he became the official who issued marriage licences. At one point he ran a distillery near York Mills. He made a large fortune over the years and died unaware that for nearly a hundred years he would be considered a great benefactor for women "of ill repute."

MERTON STREET

Davisville/Yonge
See **BALLIOL ST.**

MOATFIELD DRIVE

York Mills Rd./Leslie
See **DUNCANMILL RD.**

CTA SC 231 Item 1656

A lone carriage drives along Merton St. from Mount Pleasant in 1918.

MONTCALM AVENUE

Eglinton/Caledonia Louis-Joseph Montcalm, Marquis de Montcalm (1712–59) was the general who led the French troops against General James Wolfe and the English army in the decisive battle on the Plains of Abraham in 1759, when the French were defeated and lost their holdings in Canada. Both leaders died as a result of their wounds in that battle. Montcalm had a distinguished military career in Europe and came to Quebec in 1756. He had several notable successes in the war against the English, and was promoted to Lieutenant General in 1758, which was the second-highest position in the French army.

Montcalm disagreed violently on many issues with the Governor General, the Marquis de Vaudreuil, from whom he took his orders, and in some measure this contributed to Montcalm's final defeat on the Plains of Abraham. In 1759 the English laid siege to the city and in September 4,500 of their troops, led by Wolfe, managed to climb the cliffs. Montcalm led his troops quickly into battle, which was considered a tactical error. They were defeated, and Montcalm died the next day.

MONTGOMERY AVENUE

Yonge/Eglinton   John Montgomery's tavern gained notoriety as the Rebel headquarters in the Rebellion of 1837. Montgomery (1788–1879), who had served in the militia in the War of 1812, supported the Reformers' cause but did not approve of an armed uprising. In December 1837, when the Rebellion broke out, Montgomery was in the process of moving out of his premises in the tavern to a new house (the Willows). However, by virtue of his position as tavernkeeper, he was drawn into the Rebellion and later arrested and tried. After he was sentenced to be executed (later commuted to deportation), he gave this spirited and prophetic reply: "These perjurers ... will never die a natural death and when you, sir, and the jury shall have died and perished in hell's flames, John Montgomery will yet be living on Yonge Street." Two of the men who had falsely accused him killed themselves and Montgomery returned from exile in 1843 to rebuild his tavern (which had been burned to the ground by the Loyalist troops) and outlive all his accusers. He wasn't compensated for his loss until 1873, when Oliver Mowat's government acknowledged that his tavern and business had been worth $15,000. They gave him $3,000. See **EGLINTON AVE., FINCH AVE., WILLOWBANK BLVD.**

Death of Colonel Moodie (1889). C. W. Jeffreys. Montgomery Inn was the scene of the famous clash between Rebels and Loyalists in 1837.

MOORE AVENUE

Mount Pleasant/St. Clair   John Thomas Moore was a developer who in 1884 bought some land north of St. Clair and east of Yonge. He built his residence, Avoca Villa, at Rose Park and Inglewood. He planned to develop the area but economic conditions worked against him and he had to abandon his plans. When the area was finally built up after the First World War, it was named Moore Park in his honour. John Moore was known for his love of roses and he tended his garden carefully, importing some of his prize bushes from England. He was the founder of the Rose Society of Toronto.

MOUNT PLEASANT ROAD

Bloor to Glen Echo between Bayview and Yonge   When a road was cut through Mount Pleasant cemetery in 1916, they named it Mount Pleasant Rd. after the graveyard. The cemetery, which opened for business in 1876, was designed by Henry Engelhardt, a landscape architect who had created other cemeteries as well as public gardens throughout North America. With its winding pathways, carefully planned shrubberies and ornamental lake, the cemetery soon became one of Toronto's tourist stops. Mount Pleasant was the largest cemetery in Toronto at the time. Before 1855, people who were neither Anglican nor Catholic buried their dead in Potter's Field, a six-acre cemetery on the northwest corner of Yonge and Bloor. But the village of Yorkville was expanding and needed the land, so a new cemetery, the Necropolis, was opened at the end of Winchester St. By 1872 Toronto's growing population made it necessary to open another cemetery, and in 1873 a 200-acre farm was bought to be the future site of Mount Pleasant Cemetery.

MOWAT AVENUE

Dufferin/King   Sir Oliver Mowat (1820–1903) had a long career in federal and provincial politics, capped by his years as Premier of Ontario from 1872 until 1896. He began his career as a law student articling with Sir John A. Macdonald. He sat as a Reform (Liberal) member in the Assembly from 1848 until 1864, and was one of the Fathers of Confederation. He served as Chancellor of Ontario from 1864 until he took over as Premier in 1872. A strong and skilful leader, he presided over Ontario during a time of great change: the modernization of agriculture, widespread industrialization, improved education, the acceptance of trade unions and the introduction of social programs. Mowat was appointed Lieutenant Governor in 1897, and he died in office six years later.

MUTUAL STREET

Dundas/Jarvis

See **JARVIS ST.**

With some difficulty, hydro workers erect a hydro pole on Mutual St. in 1910.

NASSAU STREET

Bathurst/College   Ogle R. Gowan (1803–76), a Member of Parliament for Leeds County for various periods between 1836 and 1861, lived later in his life in the Kensington Market area, on the corner of what is now Nassau and

Augusta. He named his youngest son Nassau, in honour of William of Orange, King of England and the Netherlands, who belonged to the house of Nassau. Nassau was a German duchy that split in 1255 into the House of Orange (in the Netherlands) and the House of Nassau (in Germany). It is not clear whether Nassau St. was named after Nassau Gowan in particular or more generally, after the house of Nassau.

Nassau and Augusta (1978). William Sherman.

NELSON STREET

Queen/Simcoe   Horatio Nelson (1758–1805) was a naval hero whose brilliant tactics were responsible for many decisive victories for England during the Napoleonic Wars. He entered the navy when he was 12 and was a captain by the time he was 20. In a battle in 1794 off the island of Corsica, he was wounded and subsequently lost the sight in his right eye. Three years later he lost his right arm in a battle in the Canary Islands. Trafalgar Square in London is named after his famous victory just off Cape Trafalgar, where he defeated the

French and Spanish fleets but died from his wounds. A statue of Admiral Nelson stands in the middle of Trafalgar Square.

NINA STREET

Bathurst/Davenport   Nina Wells was the daughter of Frederick Wells (1822–77), who inherited the Davenport estate from his father, Colonel Joseph Wells (1773–1853). Nina, whose mother had died giving birth to her, grew up in England. She moved back to Toronto when she was 19 years old and lived in Davenport, which she had inherited when her father died. While working as a Sunday School teacher at St. Alban's Church she fell in love with the curate, Adam Urias de Pencier. They married in 1895 and lived at Davenport for 10 years. Then they moved west, first to Manitoba and then to British Columbia, where de Pencier eventually became an archbishop. See **DARTNELL AVE., DAVENPORT RD.**

OAKLANDS AVENUE

Avenue Rd./Davenport   Oaklands was a house built by John Macdonald (1824–90), a prominent citizen of Toronto who started as a clerk in a dry goods store and ended up a senator. He came from Scotland to Upper Canada when he was a teenager with his father, whose regiment was required to help squelch the 1837 Rebellion. He entered the dry goods business and eventually became the proprietor of the largest wholesale dry goods firm in the country. He built Oaklands in 1860, naming it after the many fine oak trees on the property. In those days, Avenue Rd. and Davenport was considered too far away from the city to be a convenient location for a house. Sitting on the brow of the Avenue Rd. hill, Oaklands provided a stunning view of the city and the lake. The architect William Hay designed it, creating a handsome Gothic mansion. Elected to Parliament in 1861 as a Liberal, Macdonald opposed Confederation, but nevertheless he was appointed a senator in 1887. He was a devout Methodist who supported many local institutions and he laid so many cornerstones that he had a collection of more than 30 silver trowels. After Oaklands passed out of his family's hands in 1931, the Christian Brothers transformed it into De La Salle College. Now the house is used as a residence for the Christian Brothers.

O'HARA AVENUE

TRL T 32039 JRR

Colonel Walter O'Hara commemorated famous battles in Spain when he named Roncesvalles and Sorauren avenues.

Queen/Lansdowne   Walter O'Hara (1789–1874), an Irishman who graduated from Trinity College, Dublin, joined the British army when he was 19 to fight in the Peninsular War against Napoleon. For seven years he fought with distinction, participating in all the major battles of that war under Sir Arthur Wellesley, the Duke of Wellington (1769–1852). In 1826 O'Hara came to Canada, where he was appointed the Assistant Adjutant General of the Militia. He was disappointed in his ambition to become Adjutant General, and he believed he was passed over in favour of someone with more influence. O'Hara spent years trying to persuade the authorities in London that an injustice had been done. Meanwhile, he held the position of Assistant Adjutant General until it was abolished in 1846. O'Hara was one of the first settlers to buy land in Parkdale. Between 1831 and 1840 he acquired 520 acres north of Queen and west of Dufferin. He built a red-brick Georgian home and called it West Lodge after his family estate in Ireland. When he began to subdivide his land he named many streets in the area: Roncesvalles Ave. and Sorauren Ave. after villages in Spain where he had fought in famous battles during the

Robert O'Hara painted this view of West Lodge, the house his father built just north of Queen St.

TRL T 11429 JRR

Peninsular War; Alhambra Ave. after the famous palace in Spain; Fermanagh Ave. after the county in Ireland where he was born; Marion St. after his wife; and Geoffrey and Constance streets after two of his children. After he died, West Lodge Ave. and O'Hara Ave. were laid out. See **ALHAMBRA ST., RONCESVALLES AVE., SORAUREN AVE, WELLESLEY ST.**

O'KEEFE LANE

Dundas/Yonge   Eugene O'Keefe (1827–1913) was the founder of one of the largest breweries in Canada. He came to Toronto from Ireland in 1836. In 1861 he started the Victoria Brewery in Toronto, and a year later amalgamated his company with the Hannath and Hart Brewery. By 1891, when he incorporated the O'Keefe Brewing Company, it was the largest brewer of lager beer in Canada. O'Keefe developed his lager brew using refrigeration techniques developed in the United States. In 1911, devastated by the death of his son, he sold his company and died two years later. He was a great benefactor to the Roman Catholic Church. E.P. Taylor bought the company in 1934, when it became Canadian Breweries Limited, and it was Taylor who donated the funds to build the O'Keefe Centre (renamed the Hummingbird Centre in the 1990s), just a few blocks from where O'Keefe's brewery once stood.

ORCHARD VIEW BOULEVARD

Eglinton/Yonge
See **WILLOWBANK BLVD.**

OSSINGTON AVENUE

Queen to Davenport between Bathurst and Dovercourt
See **BROOKFIELD ST.**

OTTER CRESCENT

Lawrence/Avenue Rd.   Sir William Dillon Otter (1843–1929) was a soldier for over 60 years. He began as a private with the Queen's Own Rifles in 1861 and in 1866 fought at Ridgeway during the Fenian Raids. By the time the Pilgrimage Riots and the Grand Trunk Riots broke out in 1875 and 1877 respectively, Otter was commanding his own regiment. In 1883 he directed the School of Infantry at Stanley Barracks, and during the Northwest Rebellion in 1885 he commanded the regiment that marched on Battleford to put down the Rebellion. As commander of the Royal Canadian Regiment of Infantry, Otter led the first Canadian troops sent to the Boer War in 1899. In 1908 he was made Chief of General Staff, the first Canadian to fill that position, and in 1910 he became the Inspector General of the Canadian Militia. He was knighted in 1913 and made a general in 1922.

PALACE PIER COURT

Lake Shore Blvd./Park Lawn   Toronto nearly had a pleasure pier stretching half a mile into Lake Ontario, comparable to the Steel Pier in Atlantic City and the Palace Pier in Brighton, England. Plans were drawn up in the 1920s that included a dance hall, a palace of fun, a bandstand and a theatre. Construction began, but only 300 feet were completed by the time the Depression and lack of finances put a halt to the project in 1932. In 1941 the scaled-down version finally opened its doors to the public, first as a roller rink and then as a dance hall. The big bands of the 40s and 50s played there: Les Brown, Harry James, the Dorsey Brothers, Duke Ellington, Stan Kenton, Cab Calloway, Count Basie and Trump Davidson. As musical tastes changed, Palace Pier was used for boxing matches, wrestling, high school dances and religious revivals. In 1963 an arsonist set fire to it and the whole building was destroyed. Two apartment towers were built on the site and called Palace Pier.

[Palace Pier was a popular roller-skating rink and dance hall in the 1940s and 1950s.

PALMERSTON AVENUE
PALMERSTON BOULEVARD
PALMERSTON GARDENS
PALMERSTON SQUARE

Bathurst/Bloor   Lord Henry John Temple Palmerston (1784–1865), known as "Firebrand Palmerston," was always getting into trouble, both at home and abroad, during his long political career. In 1807 he won a seat in Parliament and went on to hold several important posts, including Junior Lord of the Admiralty, Secretary of War, Foreign Secretary, Home Secretary and finally Prime Minister between 1855 and 1865. He started as a Conservative but switched to the Whigs (Liberals) in 1828. However, his policies would not be recognizably Liberal today; for example, he was against giving the vote to the working classes. A fervent British nationalist, he believed that Britain's form of responsible government would be good for everyone, and as a result he supported various European revolutions against absolute monarchies: the Paris revolution in 1830, the Italian revolution in 1848, and the Greek and Belgian wars for independence.

PARLIAMENT STREET

Lake Shore Blvd. to Bloor between Sherbourne and the Don Valley   From the outset, the lack of funds from Britain plagued the construction of the Parliament Buildings, which were built three times with long delays in between. Lieutenant Governor Simcoe planned the first Parliament Buildings, which stood just south of Front between Berkeley and Parliament. At that time Parliament St. was the eastern border of the town. There were to be two wings: one for the lower house, the Legislative Assembly, and one for the upper house, the legislative councillors, joined by a central block that would contain the governor's residence and offices. The two wings were completed by 1797 but the central block was never built. They were burned down by the invading Americans in 1813. The government had to make do with temporary accommodations, which for some time consisted of a ballroom in Jordan's Hotel on the south side of King near Berkeley. The buildings were rebuilt by 1820, but a chimney fire destroyed them in 1824. At this point it was decided that the Parliament St. location, so close to the marshy eastern harbour, was too unhealthy, and new government buildings were planned for Simcoe Place, on Front St. between Wellington, John and Simcoe. The government relocated to the York Hospital at King and John for eight years, when their new buildings were finally ready. Here the Legislature remained until the buildings at Queen's Park were completed in 1892.

The first Parliament buildings, near Front St. and Parliament, were burned down by the invading Americans in 1813.

The third Parliament buildings, near Simcoe St. and Front, were used by the legislature between 1832 and 1892.

PEARS AVENUE

Avenue Rd./Davenport   Brothers James and Leonard Pears left England in 1885 and settled in Toronto. They operated a brickmaking yard with John Townsley on the west side of Yonge St. where Pears Ave. runs today. They pronounced their name "Peers." By 1880 their company had expanded to an operation employing 60 men, but the clay in the area was nearly used up and the village of Yorkville was expanding and needed their land. The Pears moved their company to Eglinton Ave. West. In 1926 the company was sold to the city and became Eglinton Park. In its heyday, the brickyard made three million bricks a year in two colours: red and yellow. This was a popular combination for builders in the 1880s, and the company would alternate colours, making red one week and yellow the next.

PELLATT AVENUE

Albion/Weston   Sir Henry Mill Pellatt (1859–1939) was the eccentric creator of Casa Loma, the castle that sits on the Spadina hill overlooking Toronto, just south of St. Clair Ave. He was a star athlete who won the record for running the mile in 1879. A lifelong attachment to things military began when he joined the Queen's Own Rifles when he was 17. Pellatt became a successful stockbroker who was knighted in 1905 for his role in bringing electricity to Canada. He ran several electricity companies until they were nationalized by the province. Pellatt dreamed of living in a real castle and set about spending his fortune to create one. He spared no expense: the stables were the first to be completed at a cost of $200,000, with Spanish tiles, mahogany stalls and name-plates for the horses engraved in gold. The rest of the mansion developed on a lavish scale. He brought thousands of stones over from Scotland at a dollar each. An underground tunnel led from the stables to the house, where he installed all the latest conveniences and much, much more: 98 rooms, 30 bathrooms, 25 fireplaces, 5,000 electric lights, an elevator, an indoor swimming pool, a built-in vacuum-cleaning system, telephones, a shooting gallery, 3 bowling alleys and 100,000 books. He bought the property and started building in 1903, but in 1913 when he and his wife moved in, it still wasn't finished. Pellatt did everything on a grand scale, and in the end, as property taxes and his maintenance expenses rose, his bank failed and he was forced to sell Casa Loma and all its extravagant contents in 1923. He retired, and when he died in 1939 his assets totalled only $35,000. The castle was empty for a while; the city of Toronto acquired it in lieu of back taxes. Eventually the Kiwanis Club leased it in 1937 and has operated it as a tourist attraction ever since, raising money for charitable projects.

The imposing turrets of Casa Loma overlook the city below, circa 1920.

CTA SC 244 Item 4032

Sir Henry Pellatt and Lady Pellatt entertain the military at a garden party in the grounds of Casa Loma, 1919.

PEMBROKE STREET

Jarvis/Gerrard   William Herbert, the 3rd Earl of Pembroke (1580–1630), was rumoured to be the mysterious Mr. W.H., to whom Shakespeare dedicated his sonnets. Shakespeare did dedicate the first folio of his plays to Pembroke and his brother, Philip. Pembroke College, Oxford, was founded in his honour in 1624 during his term as chancellor of the University, which lasted from 1617 to 1630. Pembroke served as Lord Chamberlain in the court of James 1 from 1615 to 1625, and as Lord Steward from 1625 to 1630.

PENRYN AVENUE

Lawrence/Victoria Park   Penryn was the name of a beautiful house built by Colonel Norman D. Perry in 1932. It still stands today, on Versailles Court near York Mills and Bayview. The house was designed in Georgian Revival style by the architects Mathers and Haldenby. Penryn was a showpiece in the thirties, featured twice in the magazine *Canadian Homes and Gardens*. A drive lined with elm trees led up to the red brick and stone house. The carefully land-scaped grounds included a sunken rose garden, a 600-foot lawn and an elegant white teahouse. But Penryn has a sad history: Colonel Perry, the president of a securities corporation, killed himself by jumping off a bridge.

PETER STREET

King/Spadina   Peter St. derives its name from Petersfield, Peter Russell's country estate, which once occupied the area between Queen and Bloor, east of Spadina. After Governor Simcoe returned to England in 1796, Peter Russell (1731–1808) was the Administrator of York until 1799, when he retired. Originally from Ireland, he came to York at the age of 59 accompanied by his sister, Elizabeth. Russell had been friends with Simcoe, and he in turn encouraged his friends John Denison and William Willcocks to join him in Upper Canada. Russell built a house in town called Russell Abbey. Today Abbey Lane, near Sherbourne and Front, marks the approximate spot where it stood, overlooking Front St. and the lake. Russell acquired a great deal of land, including the lot east of Spadina where he built his farm, Petersfield. The Russells were influential members of York society at the time. When Russell died in 1808, his sister Elizabeth inherited all his property, and she left most of it to her cousins Phoebe Willcocks Baldwin and Maria Willcocks. Phoebe was married to Dr. William Baldwin, who laid out Spadina Ave. on property she had inherited from Elizabeth Russell. See **ADMIRAL RD., BALDWIN ST., BLUE JAYS WAY.**

PHOEBE STREET

Spadina/Queen
See **BALDWIN ST.**

PLAYTER BOULEVARD

Broadview/Danforth   The Playters were among the earliest settlers in York, arriving in 1796. United Empire Loyalists and Quakers, they left their home in Pennsylvania after the American Revolutionary War and lived in Kingston before moving to York. George Playter (1736–1822) and his sons, George, John, Eli and James, were each granted large lots of land, much of it in the Don Valley area. George Playter built a house on the west bank of the Don

A street sweeper pauses on Playter Blvd., with Playter House in the background, circa 1930.

River, near Castle Frank, and he constructed a bridge over the Don so he could visit his son James, who lived on the opposite side. In her diary, Elizabeth Simcoe recorded her impressions of this rough bridge, which was made from "a butternut Tree fallen across the river the branches still growing in full leaf." (Simcoe: July 6, 1796 entry) The bridge crossed the river at almost the same spot where a footbridge now spans the river near the Riverdale Farm. The Playters held various offices in the town of York over the years. During the War of 1812 they hid the town's archives and important documents in their house, along with ammunition. The Americans apparently found the archives but missed the ammunition. John Playter's eldest son, Richard, inherited the land along the Danforth where Playter Blvd. stands today. He ran a dairy farm, market gardens and orchards, as well as taking on the offices of deputy reeve and magistrate. After Richard died in 1871, one of his sons built Playter House, which can still be seen at 28 Playter Crescent. By 1915, all of the Playter property was subdivided and sold for development. See **CASTLE FRANK RD., AMELIA ST.**

POPLAR PLAINS ROAD

Avenue Rd./Dupont
See **McMASTER AVE.**

PORTLAND STREET

Bathurst/Front   The 3rd Duke of Portland was William Henry Cavendish Bentinck (1738–1809), a British statesman when the town of York was founded. He held several influential positions in his career, including Lord Lieutenant of Ireland in 1782, and Home Secretary under Prime Minister William Pitt from 1794 to 1801. From 1807 until he died in 1809 he was Prime Minister of England. Portland made the decision that York should be the site of the government of Upper Canada, despite Governor Simcoe's recommendations that a more protected spot would be preferable. Simcoe's opinion was justified in 1813, when the Americans invaded York and burned down the government buildings.

PORTNEUF COURT

Front/Sherbourne   Pierre Robineau, the Chevalier de Portneuf (1708–61) built a French fort in Toronto in the spring of 1750. He built Fort Toronto on the east bank of the Humber River, near the river's mouth, probably in the same spot where John Rousseau built his house in 1793. The fort was built to facilitate the growing fur trade, but it was found to be too small almost before it was completed, and a second fort, Fort Rouillé, was built that same year farther to the east, where the Canadian National Exhibition stands today. The competition with the English for the fur trade was fierce at this time. Portneuf built a small storehouse surrounded by a palisade, and then returned to Montreal with a load of furs. He later took charge of the garrison at Presqu'Ile. During the winter of 1757 their supplies began to run out, and Portneuf sent 44 men to live at Fort Niagara. Montcalm noted in his journal that "M. Portneuf carried too much brandy and too little flour" (Montcalm, 195–6). After the defeat of the French in 1761, Portneuf decided to return to France rather than live under the English. Unfortunately, his ship was wrecked off Cape Breton and he drowned. This street was named in the same competition in 1979 that named Albert Franck Place, Henry Lane Terrace, Douville Court, Longboat Ave and Scadding St.

POWER STREET

King/Parliament   In 1841 Upper Canada was divided into two Roman Catholic dioceses. Previous to this, one bishop had presided over the whole province, and the responsibilities were too great. The Pope appointed Michael Power (1804–47) as bishop of the western diocese. Born in Halifax to Irish parents, Power was ordained at the age of 23 and had several postings in Quebec before his consecration as bishop of the diocese of Toronto in 1842. At the time, there were 50,000 Catholics in the diocese, 3,000 of them living in Toronto, making up about one-fifth of that city's population. Power called a synod and established the ground rules for the new diocese. He travelled extensively in his diocese and began construction on St. Michael's Cathedral. The famine in Ireland in the 1840s was the catalyst for a huge wave of emigration. In 1847, 90,000 Irish disembarked at Quebec City. Many of these immigrants made their way to Toronto, bringing typhoid fever. Power caught the disease while tending to the sick, and died of it in 1847 at the age of 42.

ST. JOSEPH'S CONVENT, 1854-1863

TRL T 33440

In 1860 St. Joseph's Roman Catholic convent stood on the east side of Power St., just north of King.

PRICE STREET
PRICEFIELD ROAD

Summerhill/Yonge Joseph Price (1790–1846) came to York in 1814 from New York. Originally from Hertford, England, he bought land in York just south of today's Summerhill Ave., stretching from Yonge St. to the Don River. He established a farm and a sawmill and built a house near the corner of Rowanwood and Yonge that he called Thornwood, after his birthplace in England. Price was a captain in the militia and helped to suppress the Rebellion of 1837. After his death a portion of his land was acquired by

David MacPherson, who build Chestnut Park there. Price's daughter Sarah inherited 10 acres on Yonge St. and lived there for many years in a small cottage. A railway station, now converted into a Liquor Control Board of Ontario outlet, stands on the spot where Miss Sarah Price lived for so many years. Thornwood Rd. was named after Joseph Price's house. See **CHESTNUT PARK RD.**

PRINCE ARTHUR AVENUE

Avenue Rd./Bloor   Queen Victoria's third son, Arthur William Patrick Albert (1850–1942), served as Canada's Governor General from 1911 to 1916. He had a long military career that took him all over the world, including a stint in the Rifle Brigade in Montreal in 1870, where he saw action in the Fenian Raids. In 1874 he was created Duke of Connaught and Strathearn. Prince Arthur held the title of Commander-in-Chief of the Canadian Militia during the first two years of the First World War. He made quite a nuisance of himself, insisting that his title was more than honorary and that he be consulted about all matters concerning the war.

QUEEN STREET

Fallingbrook Rd. to Roncesvalles between King and Dundas   Until the early 1840s Queen St. was known as Lot St. It formed the northern boundary of the town and served as the base line from which the concession roads were counted and the park lots were laid out. It was renamed Queen St. in 1844 in honour of Queen Victoria (b. 1819, r. 1837–1901). Victoria St. was named in the same year. Alexandrina Victoria of the House of Hanover became Queen in 1837 when her uncle William IV died. Her father, Edward, the Duke of Kent, was the fourth son of George III, and her mother was a German princess, Victoria Mary Louisa of Saxe-Coburg-Gotha. The baby princess was the first member of the royal family to be vaccinated. She was not told that she was heir to the throne until she was 12, and there was a rumour that William IV held off dying until she came of age, just for spite so her mother wouldn't become Regent. Lord Melbourne, who was Prime Minister when Victoria became Queen, served as her chief adviser during the first years of her reign. As she gained experience, her influence grew, but she always relied heavily upon advice from her Cabinet ministers, especially Benjamin Disraeli (Prime Minister from 1874 to 1880), who was a great favourite of hers. Victoria married her first cousin, Prince Albert of Saxe-Coburg-Gotha, in 1840 and had nine children. His death in 1861 sent her into a prolonged period of mourning. Victoria ruled Britain longer than any other monarch (64 years). During her reign Britain enjoyed growing prosperity and influence abroad: Queen Victoria became Empress of India in 1876. Industry developed and the population doubled. Victoria brought a new respectability and order to the English royal family, and came to symbolize the peace and prosperity of her age. See **ALBERT ST., ALBERTA AVE., CLARENCE SQUARE, MELBOURNE AVE.**

TRL T 12757

These shops on Queen St. W. were demolished in 1887 to make way for the new City Hall.

RADISSON STREET

Eglinton/McCowan   Pierre-Esprit Radisson (1636–1710) was a fur trader and explorer who teamed up with his brother-in-law, Médard Chouart des Groseilliers in 1659 to seek out new supplies of furs in the area around Lake Superior and Lake Michigan. He had already spent time living among the Iroquois, which proved valuable on his many fur-trading expeditions. The governor of New France at the time punished Radisson and Groseilliers for setting out without permission, so they switched allegiance and began to work for the British, who financed an expedition to Hudson's Bay on the ship *Nonesuch* in 1668 and 1669. Radisson's and Groseilliers' plan was to bypass the French and the St. Lawrence River, and bring the furs directly to Europe via Hudson's Bay. The Hudson's Bay Company was born and Radisson established its first post at Nelson River in 1670. Radisson grew unhappy with his British masters and went back to the French in 1674, but he was never fully trusted, and he returned to the English to run Hudson Bay's post at Fort Nelson from 1685 to 1687. Then he retired to England (there was a price on his head in Canada!) and wrote up his adventures.

RAGLAN AVENUE

Bathurst/St. Clair   Lord Raglan, Fitzroy James Henry Somerset (1788–1855) had a distinguished military career serving under the Duke of Wellington in the Napoleonic Wars, as military secretary and aide-de-camp. He lost his right arm as a result of wounds he sustained in the Battle of Waterloo in 1815. After Wellington died in 1852, Raglan was promoted to general and put in charge of the troops sent to the Crimea in 1854. He commanded the troops at the battles of Balaclava and Inkerman in 1854. The war went very badly, with enormous suffering on the part of the troops. There weren't enough supplies of food and clothing and some military decisions were catastrophic (e.g., the Charge of the Light Brigade). Much of the blame fell on Raglan's shoulders and he took it very hard. In 1855 he died near Sebastopol as a result of dysentery. He left his name on a style of sleeve his soldiers wore in that war: raglan sleeves. See **INKERMAN ST.**

RATHNELLY AVENUE

Avenue Rd./Dupont
See **McMASTER AVE.**

REBECCA STREET

Queen/Ossington   The name of this street originates from the Rebeccaites of South Wales, who protested against paying tolls by destroying tollgates in 1843. Their name came from a reference to a gate in the *Bible*, Genesis 24:60: "Rebecca ... let thy seed possess the gate of those which hate them." Rebecca St. was used as an alternative route to avoid the tollgate at Queen and Ossington. There had been many disputes between the road trustees and a contractor who transported wood along Dundas and down to the garrison near Lake Ontario. Every time his workers passed through the toll they had to pay. This caused a good deal of ill-feeling between the contractor's employees and the keepers of the gate, and continual quarrels took place – even to the point of violence. Eventually the contractor bought the plot of ground where Rebecca St. now runs and cut a lane through it, bypassing the toll.

REES STREET

Spadina/Lake Shore Blvd.   William Rees (1800–74) was a doctor with a sense of mission who was chiefly responsible for the creation of the Provincial Lunatic Asylum in 1841. Born in Bristol, England, he came to Canada as a young doctor in 1819 and served as the assistant health officer at the port of Quebec. He moved to York in 1829 and set up a medical practice. He held strong convictions about social reform and put his theories into practice by offering free vaccinations and medical advice for the poor. Rees supported many causes over the years. His interests included the establishment of various social institutions such as orphanages, juvenile reformatories and alcoholic treatment centres, as well as a system of health inspectors, a provincial museum, a city waterworks and a street railway. His most successful project was the Provincial Lunatic Asylum, founded in 1841. He became the Asylum's medical superintendent and researched the latest methods of treatment in Europe at his own expense. In 1844 one of his inmates attacked him and he suffered a serious head injury. His eyesight was damaged and he could no longer work. He applied for a pension and compensation but his only payment from the legislature was $1,000, paid out in 1864. He lived the balance of his life in a cottage on the waterfront, near where Rees St. runs today.

RICHMOND STREET

Sumach to Strachan between King and Queen   The 4th Duke of Richmond and Lennox came to Canada in 1818 to assume the position of Governor-in-Chief of British North America. Charles Lennox (1764–1819) joined the militia as a young man and rose through the ranks to the position of Lieutenant-Colonel. He was elected to Parliament in 1790, taking his father's seat. In 1806 he inherited the title of Duke when his uncle died, and then from 1807 until 1813 served as the Lord Lieutenant of Ireland. His attitude to the Roman Catholics was one of inflexibility, but his love of sports and hunting ensured him a certain level of popularity. In Canada he showed a similar political rigidity, and laid the ground for future conflict by insisting that the Executive be financially independent from the Assembly. Here again, however, his love of sports and recreation drew him support from the elite. He set a number of plans in motion during his short term: notably the construction of canals and roads. He set out in the summer of 1819 to tour Upper and Lower Canada but contracted rabies after being bitten by a rabid fox and died. Richmond's son-in-law was Sir Peregrine Maitland, who was appointed Lieutenant Governor of Upper Canada in 1818. See **MAITLAND ST.**

These stores at Richmond and Yonge were torn down in 1899 when Simpson's was built.

ROBERT STREET

College/Spadina   This street was laid out in 1873 by Robert Baldwin, the son of Robert Baldwin (1804–58), a leading Reformer who worked tirelessly in his political life to bring responsible government to Upper Canada. Whether he named it after his father, himself, or his great-grandfather (another Robert Baldwin), is not entirely clear. However, his father played a key role in the history of government in Canada and deserves some mention here. From a distance of nearly 150 years, a look at Robert Baldwin's life presents a fascinating picture of a complicated, troubled man who strove to do his duty as a public figure while struggling with shyness, introspection and crippling depression. Baldwin's fragile happiness depended on his wife, who unfortunately died

Robert Baldwin was buried with his wife's letters placed over his heart and his coffin chained to hers.

young after only nine years of marriage. She died several months after a difficult Caesarean birth. Baldwin was devastated and never completely recovered
from his grief. When he died he left specific instructions with his daughter,
Maria, which involved placing his wife's letters over his heart and chaining
their coffins together. He also wanted an incision made in his corpse that
would match the Caesarean incision his wife had endured. Maria did all that
he asked, but drew the line at the incision. His son Willcocks discovered his
father's written request a month after his funeral, and struck by the solemn
pleading therein, arranged for his father's body to be exhumed and the incision
to be made. Despite Baldwin's melancholy and emotionally disturbed outlook,
he made an important contribution to the development of democracy and
responsible government in Canada. As a member of the Legislative Assembly,
and then the Executive Council, he worked steadily as a Reformer against the
Family Compact. He resigned several times as a matter of conscience. The first
time was with the other councillors in 1836 when Lieutenant Governor
Francis Bond Head refused to consult the very officers he had appointed. This
crisis was one of the catalysts for the Rebellion of 1837, in which Baldwin took
no part. But after the Rebellion Baldwin emerged as a leader for the
Reformers. His character, marked by his qualities of honesty and devotion to
duty and principle, drew him great respect and influence. He was Solicitor
General under Sydenham and resigned again in 1841 when that gentlemen
refused to implement responsible government. Baldwin worked with Louis-
Hippolyte LaFontaine, the leader of the Liberals in Lower Canada and
together they were elected to form a government in 1842 and again in 1848.
Their government from 1848 to 1851 passed many of their goals into law.
Responsible government was ensured and the judiciary system reformed. The
Rebellion Losses bill was passed to recompense Reformers who had property
damaged during the Rebellion. Baldwin resigned in 1851 and was defeated
when he ran again. Depression and ill health plagued him and he died in 1858.
Baldwin made great achievements in the political arena, despite the emotional
torment he lived with for most of his life. See **BALDWIN ST., BOND ST.,
SYDENHAM ST., WALMER RD.**

ROLYAT STREET

Dundas/Ossington
See **BROOKFIELD ST.**

RONCESVALLES AVENUE

Dundas/Bloor   Roncesvalles is a small village in northern Spain in the Pyrenees near the French border. Colonel Walter O'Hara fought in a battle there during the Peninsular War against Napoleon. O'Hara was one of the earliest landowners in Parkdale. Roncesvalles is also known as the site where Charlemagne's legendary paladin Roland was said to have been killed in 778. *The Song of Roland* was an early French epic that described the battle and Roland's death. Charlemagne (742–814) was the king of the Franks who conquered most of Europe and was crowned Emperor by the Pope on Christmas Day, 800. It is hard to separate legend from history, but it seems that Charlemagne left a rearguard to fight at Roncesvalles. They were surrounded by Saracens and Count Hruodland (who later became known as Roland) was killed. See **O'HARA AVE.**

CTA RG 8 Series 58 Item 815

Laying streetcar tracks along Roncesvalles.

ROSEDALE ROAD
ROSEDALE HEIGHTS DRIVE
ROSEDALE VALLEY ROAD

Bloor/Yonge; St. Clair/Mount Pleasant; Bloor/Mount Pleasant   In 1827, when Mary Boyles Powell married William Botsford Jarvis (1799–1864), she moved into the house he had bought from John Small three years before. Because it stood on the edge of a ravine, on a hillside covered in wild roses, Mary called it Rosedale. Soon the house needed some additions to accommodate their growing family, so they hired John Howard (the architect who eventually donated High Park to the city) to design two new wings, adding a morning

In this 1835 drawing James Hamilton captured the sylvan charm of the Jarvis property, Rosedale.

room, a conservatory, a grapery, a peach house and some new bedrooms. A long verandah was built across the front. Then Mary set about taming the wilderness by landscaping the grounds with orchards, pathways, formal rose gardens and picturesque arbours. William Jarvis, second cousin to Samuel Peters Jarvis, who lived closer to town at Hazel Burn, held the position of High Sheriff of the Home District from 1827 to 1856. During the Rebellion of 1837, William Lyon Mackenzie wanted to burn down Rosedale, but Samuel Lount, who knew William Jarvis, prevented it. One of Jarvis' most difficult duties came after the Rebellion, when he had to supervise Lount's execution. The story goes that when he started to cry in his distress at hanging his friend, Lount hugged him and then kissed him goodbye. Rosedale stood just south of Cluny Drive on Rosedale Rd. It was demolished in 1905. The suburb originally was called Rose Park when it was laid out in the 1850s by William's nephew, Edgar Jarvis, but in later years it came to be known as Rosedale. See **LOUNT ST., HIGHLAND AVE., EDGAR AVE.**

ROSEHILL AVENUE

Yonge/St. Clair In 1835, Jesse Ketchum gave his daughter Ann and her husband, Walter Rose, a piece of land that ran from Yonge St. to Bayview Ave., just south of St. Clair. Ketchum built them a house and they called it Rose Hill. Joseph Jackes bought it in 1865. See **JACKES AVE.**

RUNNYMEDE ROAD

Bloor/Jane John Scarlett, a landowner and businessman who owned a huge chunk of land in the area north of Bloor and west of Keele St., built a house in 1838 on the corner of Dundas and Keele and called it Runnymede. Runnymede was the famous meadow on the south bank of the Thames, about 20 miles southwest of London, where King John signed the Magna Carta in 1215. See **SCARLETT RD.**

RUSHOLME DRIVE
RUSHOLME PARK CRESCENT
RUSHOLME ROAD

College/Dovercourt   For 114 years, from 1839 until 1953, a house called
Rusholme near Dovercourt and College was occupied by the same family, the
Denisons. George Taylor Denison II (1816–96) was the second son of George
Taylor Denison (1783–1853), who lived at Belle Vue. Denison II, who had a
career in law and the military, built Rusholme in 1839. He named it after a
property in Manchester, England, which belonged to a relative, Joseph
Denison. The driveway curved up to the house from Dundas and Rusholme.
He had married Mary Anne Dewson the year before, and soon they filled their
house with children. Dewson St. is named after Mary Anne. George supported
the Confederate army in the American Civil War and at one point, General
Robert E. Lee visited Rusholme. They had lots of other important visitors,
including members of the royal family. Elegant parties and balls were held at

George Taylor Denison II, seated at right, with his family on the steps of Rusholme in 1871.

Rusholme, and George's daughters were presented at court. In the 1850s he began to subdivide his land and by 1884 the estate was reduced to a small block of land around the house. George's eldest son, George Taylor Denison III (1839–1925) built his own house nearby in 1864 and called it Heydon Park. George's second son, Frederick, inherited Rusholme and lived there until his death in 1896. His son lived there until he died in 1953, and then the house was sold and demolished. See **BELLEVUE AVE., BROOKFIELD ST., DENISON AVE., DOVERCOURT RD., HEYDON PARK RD.**

The Denison family occupied Rusholme from 1839 until 1953. Circa 1895.

RUSSELL STREET
RUSSELL HILL DRIVE
RUSSELL HILL ROAD

College/Spadina; Spadina/St. Clair; Avenue Rd./St. Clair   All these streets were named after Peter Russell (1731–1808), the first Administrator of the town of York, and his sister, Elizabeth Russell. See **ADMIRAL RD., BALDWIN ST., PETER ST.**

RYERSON AVENUE

Bathurst/Queen   Adolphus Egerton Ryerson (1803–82) laid the foundations for the public education system in Ontario. Born into a Loyalist Anglican family, he converted to Methodism as a young man and was ordained in 1827. A man of strong religious and political opinions, Ryerson supported the Reformers, although he disapproved of William Lyon Mackenzie's extremism and the violence that erupted in 1837. Ryerson edited the *Christian Guardian*, and in 1826 denounced the all-pervading influence of the Anglican Church in Upper Canada. In 1841 he became the first principal of Victoria College, and from 1874 to 1878 served as president of the Methodist Church of Canada. His appointment as superintendent of education in Canada West resulted in

TRL T 30149

Egerton Ryerson's Normal School set the standard for education in Ontario. Circa 1870.

profound changes in education. Ryerson established the Normal School in 1852, a school for training teachers. Ryerson believed in free education for everyone, and was convinced that humanity's salvation would be achieved through religion and universal education. He was instrumental in the passing of the School Act of 1871, which laid out the principles on which Ontario's school system is now based.

ST. CLAIR AVENUE

Kingston Rd. to Scarlett Rd. between Bloor/Danforth and Eglinton   St. Clair Ave. got its name by accident and a spelling mistake. The Grainger family owned a market garden and florist shop on Yonge St. near St. Clair in the second half of the 19th century. They lived on a farm near Avenue Rd. and St. Clair. One of the Grainger children, Albert, didn't have a middle name and decided to give himself a name from his favourite book, *Uncle Tom's Cabin* by Harriet Beecher Stowe. The name he chose was "St. Clare," the hero who had bought

CTA SC 244 Item 1096

Looking south on Avenue Rd. from St. Clair at a budding traffic jam, 1937.

Uncle Tom and set him free. *Uncle Tom's Cabin* toured throughout North America as a play, and in the program the name was often misspelt as "St. Clair." So Albert adopted this version of the name, and in fun painted it on a sign and nailed it to a tree on his farm. He was a bugler with the Queen's Own Rifles and often performed with the military band at the Opera House, where he found his nickname useful as an alias when he was dating showgirls. Albert died at the age of 20 in 1872, apparently from the complications of a cold he caught while drilling with his regiment. But his sign remained nailed to the tree, and when surveyors came to map out the road, they took it for a street sign and called the second concession St. Clair Ave. The name came originally from the Italian saint, St. Clare, who was an ardent follower of St. Francis in the 13th century, and founded an order of Franciscan nuns called the "Poor Clares." They gave up all rights to property and begged for alms, living together as a contemplative order that spent much of their time in Holy Silence. The order survived the Middle Ages and the Industrial Revolution: as of 1989 there were 700 Houses of Poor Clares throughout the world. In 1913 a Roman Catholic community in Toronto raised the money for their own church and built it near Dufferin on St. Clair Ave. West. They named their church after the saint, and spelled it correctly: St. Clare's Church.

Looking east at St. Clair and Dufferin, 1928.

ST. GEORGE STREET

Bloor/Spadina   Laurent Quetton St. George (1771–1821) was an exiled French Royalist who fought against the Republicans in the French Revolution and managed to escape to England. He adopted the English name "St. George" because he had arrived in England on St. George's Day, April 23. The British government offered the French exiles land grants in Upper Canada, so St. George set off to make a new life in North America. He began by trading furs and established connections with Objibwas and fur merchants in New York and Montreal. Then he moved to York and set up shop as a merchant. He traded in furs and sold all kinds of goods, both local and imported. He also provided financial services for his customers. St. George, although never fully accepted by the social elite in York, soon proved himself an astute businessman, opening up several branch stores in other communities. He was so successful that he built himself a large house at the corner of King and Frederick streets. The house was the first brick house to be built in York,

TRL T 11482

Quetton St. George built this handsome house on King St. E. near Frederick in 1811. Circa 1885.

made from bricks imported from the United States. St. George made friends with Dr. William Warren Baldwin, who named one of his sons after him, and when Baldwin opened up Spadina Ave. and the streets around it in 1836, he named one of the streets St. George. After King Louis XVIII came to the throne in 1815, St. George returned to France, where the King made him a Chevalier to honour his loyalty in the past. He bought land there with some of the considerable fortune he had acquired in Upper Canada and died at the age of 50. See **BALDWIN ST.**

ST. GERMAIN AVENUE

Yonge/Lawrence   Alfred Hyacinthe St. Germain (1827–1908) owned 200 acres west of Yonge and north of Lawrence in 1883, and lived in a farm just north of Lawrence on Yonge. He had been the owner of several newspapers, starting with the *Kingston Herald*, and then the *Christian Journal* when he moved to Toronto in 1860. In 1861 he started a new paper, the *Toronto Evening Journal*. It started out as a weekly, but in 1864 St. Germain converted it into a daily and sold it for a penny. This was an innovation in the Toronto newspaper business, where newspapers were subscribed to and delivered with the post. He attracted advertisers by charging low rates. His readership was said to be 5,000 when the paper closed in 1866. St. Germain claimed that he was descended from one of Jacques Cartier's companions, Rudolf St. Germain.

SCADDING AVENUE

AO S 677

Rev. Henry Scadding wrote a captivating history of early Toronto filled with rambling reminiscences.

Front/Parliament   This is another street in the St. Lawrence Neighbourhood that was named in the competition of 1979. Henry Scadding (1813–1901), a historian and author, provided many of the stories in this book. In 1873 he wrote *Toronto of Old*, a rambling reminiscence and history of the city up to the year 1834, filled with personal anecdotes. This book has served as a source book for Toronto history for over a hundred years. Henry was the youngest son of John Scadding (1754–1824), who was John Graves Simcoe's property manager in Devonshire. After Simcoe's appointment as Lieutenant Governor in 1792, Scadding decided to follow Simcoe to Upper Canada. Scadding was granted 200 acres just east of the Don River between the lake and Danforth Ave. He built a log cabin but then returned with Simcoe to England in 1796, where he continued to manage his property. Scadding married and in 1821 came back to York with his wife and three sons. They lived in a farmhouse on a hill above the river very close to the spot where the Don Jail now stands, near Gerrard and Broadview. Scadding, who was an experienced property manager, soon planted his fields with wheat, barley, rye, oats and corn. He set his sheep to graze in the meadowland by the river and planted orchards, flower gardens and a respectable vegetable patch. He is credited for introducing rhubarb to the area. He died in an accident in 1824, when a tree that was being cut down on his property fell on him. Henry Scadding was the first pupil to be enrolled at Upper Canada College, and went on to university in England at St. John's College, Cambridge, where he received his Doctor of Divinity in 1832. He returned to York to teach classics at his old school, and eventually was named rector of a new church, Holy Trinity. He lived at 10 Trinity Square, a tall, narrow house, which was named Scadding House and still stands beside the church, both now dwarfed by the Eaton Centre a few yards away. Henry Scadding was one of the founders of the York Pioneer and Historical Society in 1869 and served as its president from 1880 until 1898. He contributed to two other books about Toronto's history: *Toronto, Past & Present* (1884) by John Charles Dent, and *Toronto, Old & New* (1891) by Mercer Adam. Scadding's legacy to Toronto is *Toronto of Old*, in which he walks the reader through the streets of 1834 York, pointing out this person's house and that person's store, describing the circumstances of their lives. It provides a vivid and affectionate picture of the early town. John Scadding's original cabin was preserved and moved to the Exhibition Grounds in 1879, where it remains today. See **ALBERT FRANCK PLACE, DOUVILLE COURT, HENRY LANE TERRACE, LONGBOAT AVE., PORTNEUF COURT.**

SCARLETT ROAD

Eglinton/Jane John Scarlett (1777–1865) owned over 1,000 acres north of Bloor and west of Keele. He came to York from England in 1808 and married Mary Thomson. She was a close friend of Elizabeth Russell, who was sister to Peter Russell, who had been the Administrator of York and a prominent figure in York society at the time. Scarlett started with a grist mill on the east shore of the Humber River, but over the years he operated several business ventures, including a sawmill, brickyards, a lumberyard and a distillery. He loved horses and in 1837 built a racetrack near Dundas and Weston Rd. It closed after four years. He built a house in 1838 on Dundas and Keele and called it Runnymede.

"Scarlett's Road" ran north from his property beside the Humber River. In the late 1840s Scarlett started to divide up his property, and in the 1850s the railway came and the area was ripe for subdivision. One of the first areas to be laid out was called Runnymede Estate. Because he was the first settler there and owned such a great deal of land, as well as being the only employer in the area for many years, John Scarlett was referred to as the "Father of the Junction." The neighbourhood around Dundas and Keele became known as the Junction after the railway station opened there in 1884. See **KEELE ST., PETER ST., RUNNYMEDE RD.**

SCOTT LANE
SCOTT STREET

Front/Yonge   Thomas Scott (1746–1824) lived in a house near Front and Yonge, where Scott St. and Scott Lane are located today. Born in Scotland, Scott worked as a tutor for some time before studying law in London and qualifying as a lawyer in 1793. When he was 54 he managed to secure an appointment in Upper Canada, and he came to York in 1800 as the Attorney General. He went on to hold other influential positions: he was appointed to the Executive Council in 1805, the Legislative Council in 1806, and was made Chief Justice that same year. In those early days, the processing and administration of land claims were ongoing problems and Scott presided over the chaos with varying degrees of success. He tried to retire for five years and finally was awarded a pension in 1816 and left public office with a sigh of relief.

SEVERN STREET

Davenport/Yonge   John Severn (1807–80) operated a successful brewery in the Rosedale ravine from 1832 until 1880, very close to where Severn St. is today. He started out as a blacksmith in his native Derbyshire, in England, and emigrated to Canada in 1830, where he continued to ply his trade in the town of York. He moved north to the community of Yorkville in 1832 and bought a brewery from a man named John Baxter. Severn resuscitated the brewery and soon made a success of it. By 1867 he was turning out between 6,000 and 7,000 gallons of ale and porter a week. Over the years Severn opened other breweries in California and Iowa, but he returned to his brewery in Yorkville in 1863. Severn was one of the first councillors for the new village of Yorkville in 1853, and he is represented on the Yorkville coat of arms by the letter "S" and a keg of beer. This coat of arms can be seen above the door on the firehall on Yorkville Ave. Severn served as reeve of Yorkville from 1868 until 1877. He is buried in Mount Pleasant Cemetery under an unusual monument of red granite with six pillars holding up a large dome of granite. The pillars were rumoured to represent his family: Severn, three wives and two children. His wives and children all predeceased him. See **COTTINGHAM RD., CUMBERLAND ST.**

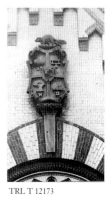

TRL T 12173

The Yorkville coat of arms celebrated the first town councillors, including a barrel for Severn, the brewer.

TRL T 10907

In 1867 John Severn's brewery produced between 6,000 and 7,000 gallons of ale and porter a week.

SHAW STREET

Dundas/Ossington   This street was named after Aeneas Shaw, the Captain-Lieutenant who commanded the first detachment of the Queen's Rangers in York in 1792. He supervised the initial clearing of land and building of the garrison, and built a log cabin for himself and his family near Dundas and Ossington in the dense forest that covered that part of the city. Shaw was born in Scotland and emigrated to New York in 1770. He joined the Queen's Rangers and fought with the British during the American Revolution, then moved to Nova Scotia, where he became a successful farmer. When the Rangers were reorganized for service in Upper Canada, he joined up again and set off to lead his men to that distant wilderness. Shaw was appointed to the Executive Council in 1794, and took a seat in the Legislative Council at the same time. His administrative skills were needed in the fledgling community, and he gave his support to the Administrator, Peter Russell. In 1811, during a time of growing tensions between the United States and the Canadas, Shaw was promoted to Major General and given the responsibility of training the troops, no easy task considering many were volunteers who could only be trained for three days in a row before they went back to their civilian lives. He commanded the troops that tried to defend York against the American invasion in April 1813 but he was far past his prime as a soldier and made several tactical errors. Shaw died in 1814.

SHEARD STREET

Carlton/Yonge   Joseph Sheard (1813–83) was an architect who designed several buildings in Toronto between 1846 and 1861. He came to Upper Canada from Yorkshire, England in 1833. He had been trained as a wheelwright in England, and worked first as a carpenter, then as a builder in Upper Canada. By 1846 he had established himself as an architect and designed schools, banks and private homes. Sheard designed the William Cawthra house at King and Bay in 1852, and a house for Oliver Mowat on Jarvis Street in 1856. (Mowat, who was one of the Fathers of Confederation, became Premier of Ontario in

1872, and Lieutenant Governor in 1897.) Sheard's last big project was the Ontario Bank at Wellington and Scott streets, in 1861. Then he handed his business over to his son-in-law, William Irving, and devoted more time to politics, in which he had been involved all along. He held the position of alderman for some time and then in 1871 he was elected mayor of Toronto. See **MOWAT AVE.**

SHELDRAKE BOULEVARD

Eglinton/Yonge   There are still traces in this area of the family that once owned a considerable amount of property here: the Stibbards. Sheldrake Blvd. and Stibbard Ave. were both named after John Sheldrake Stibbard (1840–1925). Sherwood Park occupies land he donated to the city for a park, and 394 Sheldrake and 86 Stibbard were both houses built by the family. Fruit trees from John Stibbard's orchards still grow in some gardens on Sheldrake Blvd. He operated a market garden in this area, from a farmhouse located approximately where the Eglinton United Church is today, at 65 Sheldrake. His other major occupation was the operation of an early transportation system on Yonge St.: a horse-drawn streetcar. After it was replaced by more modern vehicles, the coach served as a henhouse behind his house at 394 Sheldrake. John's father, Robert Stibbard Sr., came to Upper Canada from England in 1835, and evidence suggests that he was one of the rebels who were tied together and herded down Yonge St. after the failed Rebellion in 1837. After he was released (as many of the men were, for lack of evidence), he established himself as a market gardener and cabinetmaker. His wife's name was Sheldrake, a combination of the names Sheldon and Drake; her family claimed to have been descended from Sir Francis Drake. One of their daughters, Laura, married into the Grainger family, who owned a florist business in Deer Park and were responsible for the naming of St. Clair Ave. The other son, Robert Stibbard Jr., took over his father's farm in 1885. When one of Robert's daughters got married, he built her a house at the corner of Mount Pleasant and Sheldrake for $200. The house was referred to for years as "the Chocolate Drop" because of its dark brown paint. See **LOUNT ST., MONTGOMERY AVE., ST. CLAIR AVE.**

SHEPPARD AVENUE

Kingston Rd. to Weston Rd. between Ellesmere/York Mills/Wilson and Finch

There is some doubt as to which Sheppard this street was named after, because two of them lived on opposite corners of the intersection of Yonge and Sheppard. On the southwest corner stood the Golden Lion Hotel, established in 1824 by Tom Shepherd (sometimes spelled Sheppard). In 1856 his son Charles took over the inn, which he operated until 1870, when he sold it. On the northwest corner, a very early resident, Joseph Shepard, built a log house in 1802. His youngest son, Joseph, built a much more substantial house and store there later on, with red bricks hauled up Yonge St. by oxen from Yorkville. Joseph Shepard Sr., who died in 1837 just before the Rebellion broke out, started his life in Canada as a fur trader in 1774. When the town of York was laid out by Governor Simcoe in 1793, Shepard was one of the men who helped to build the first rough log houses on the townsite. In 1802 he

Tom Shepherd ran the Golden Lion Hotel on the southwest corner of Yonge and Sheppard, shown here in the 1890s.

bought a large farm property in the Yonge/Sheppard area, where he built his own log cabin. In 1805 he took on the job of highway overseer and fence-viewer for Yonge St. between York Mills and Steeles. Shepard suffered severe injuries in the 1813 invasion of York, but he managed to recover. He went on to build a large sawmill on the west branch of the Don River at Bathurst St. The road to this mill from Yonge and his farmhouse became known as Shepard Avenue. In 1817 he donated the land for St. John's York Mills Anglican Church, and in 1835 he built a bigger house at 90 Burndale Ave., which is still standing. Shepard passed on his farm and his mills (he also built one on the east branch of the Don near Leslie) to his sons Thomas and Michael. All the Shepards, father and sons, were active in the Reform movement and supported William Lyon Mackenzie. One son, Michael, was pardoned in 1843 for his participation in the Rebellion.

SHEPPARD STREET

Bay/Queen   This little street was once the location of an axe factory run by Harvey Shepard, an ironworker who came to York from New England. At first Shepard sold his wares from a small shop on King St., but the fine quality of his axes soon ensured his success in his adopted country, and he moved to a larger factory on the west side of the street that later became known as Shepard St. In 1838 his factory was taken over by Thomas Campion, from Sheffield, England.

SHERBOURNE STREET

Dundas/Jarvis   The town of Sherborne in Dorset, England, was the home of the Ridout family before they immigrated to North America. The elder Ridout, Thomas, came with his family to York in the 1790s from Virginia and found occupation in the administration of the new town in various positions, including Surveyor General and Registrar. The Ridout family was unfortunately connected to two of the famous duels of the early 1800s. John Ridout, one of Thomas' sons, was killed in a duel by Samuel Peters Jarvis in 1817. Samuel Ridout (b. 1778), an older brother, bought Attorney General John White's park lot in 1818. White was killed in a duel with his neighbour,

John Small, in 1800, and buried in his backyard. Samuel's property ran from Queen to Bloor, between Sherbourne and Seaton. He sold part of his land to his brother, Thomas Gibbs Ridout, who held the respected position of cashier in the Bank of Upper Canada. In 1845 Thomas and his neighbour, William Allan, came to an agreement to open a road between their two properties, with Allan contributing a 20-foot strip of land and Samuel giving up a 30-foot strip. Samuel asked that the street be named "Sherborne" in honour of his family's origins. As with many of the old street names in Toronto, the spelling changed inexplicably. Thomas sold most of his land along Sherbourne but kept a section between Carlton and Howard, where in 1857 he started to build an extremely grand mansion he dubbed Sherborne Villa. Unfortunately, the Bank of Upper Canada failed and he had to sell off his property and beautiful house. He died in 1861. The house survived for over 100 years until 1964, with various rich and influential owners, including Henry S. Howland and Senator George Cox. At one point it was converted into a residence for female employees at Simpson's Department Store. See **BERKELEY ST., HOMEWOOD AVE., JARVIS ST.**

The elegant Sherborne Villa was built by a banker in 1857 who shortly afterwards faced financial ruin and had to sell it.

CTA SC 244 Item 3120

SHOULDICE COURT

Leslie/York Mills   This little street is named after a doctor who developed an internationally acclaimed treatment for hernias and established a clinic that specialized in hernia operations. Earle Shouldice, who died in 1965, graduated from the University of Toronto medical program in 1916 and taught medicine for 25 years. During the Second World War, he grew interested in curing hernias. Many healthy men were rejected for active service because of this condition. Shouldice, who worked as a consulting physician to the army, began treating his patients for no charge, and he opened the Shouldice Clinic after the war in a little house on Church St. His methods and success became famous and in 1953 he bought a large house and large, attractive, wooded property near Bayview and Steeles, where he soon opened a much larger clinic, which continues to thrive. Over the years, over 200,000 patients have been treated for hernias at the Shouldice Clinic.

SIFTON COURT

Bayview/Sheppard   Clifford Sifton (1861–1929) had an interesting political career, capped by his knighthood in 1915. His greatest achievement was his campaign to attract settlers to farm on the prairies between 1896 and 1905. He took the controversial route of recruiting immigrants from Eastern Europe as well as the United States and Britain. Sifton began his political life in Brandon, Manitoba, where he practised law. In 1888 he entered provincial politics, quickly rising to the position of Attorney General by 1891. Despite a problem with his hearing that he struggled with for most of his life, he proved to be a masterful politician with brilliant analytical skills and dynamic energy. In 1896 he moved to federal politics, where he was appointed Minister of the Interior and Superintendent General of Indian Affairs in Wilfrid Laurier's government. In this capacity he launched his ambitious plan to settle the prairies. In 1905 Sifton had a major disagreement with Laurier regarding the role of the federal government in education. He resigned as minister, and in 1911 his opposition to Laurier's policy of reciprocity (free trade with the United States) led to his changing his allegiance to the Conservatives under Robert Laird Borden. Sifton didn't run for Parliament after this. He was a very rich man with considerable financial interests, including the ownership of

William James Topley
NAC PA 027943

Despite a lifelong hearing disability, Clifford Sifton enjoyed a dynamic political career.

the *Manitoba Free Press*. In 1924 he bought some land at Bayview and Lawrence and built three grand houses: one for himself, and two more for members of his family. They all loved riding, so Sifton built riding stables and a riding school in the Don Valley just north of his house. Today, his house at 318 Lawrence Ave. East is the Toronto French School. Sifton had a heart attack and died in 1929 in New York, on his way back to Canada from his winter home in Florida. He left an estate of $10 million. See **LAIRD DR., LAURIER AVE.**

SIMCOE STREET

TRL T 34632

John Graves Simcoe imposed a particularly British sensibility on the new settlement at York.

Queen/University   John Graves Simcoe (1752–1806), the founder of York, was the first Lieutenant Governor of Upper Canada. All three of his names were used for street names. The original Simcoe St. ran between Spadina and Niagara and is now part of Richmond St. The present Simcoe St. used to be Graves St., but the cemetery connotation proved too strong for public taste and it was renamed Simcoe. Before Duncan St. was inserted between them, John St. and Graves St. used to be adjacent. Although Simcoe founded York, he spent a relatively short time here: from 1793 to 1796. But in that time he laid the foundations for the city that is Toronto today. Simcoe's most visible legacy is the grid system of Toronto's streets, with their north/south, east/west orientation. This military approach completely ignored the topography of the site: the streams, rivers, ravines and hills. Simcoe, who had commanded the Queen's Rangers during the American Revolution, chose the site of York for the capital of Upper Canada because of its strategic location. In some degree, Simcoe's approach to government and granting land to government officials set the scene for the Rebellion in 1837. He organized a system of lots and land grants with the intention of creating a landed gentry similar to the English model. Many of his friends and associates were among the first to receive appointments and choice lots. He wanted to firmly establish British government and social institutions, hoping to attract American settlers unsatisfied with the new regime there. With this in mind he discouraged elected town meetings (such as were practised in New England), abolished slavery, established a court of justice (the Court of King's Bench) and encouraged municipal councils, the founding of preparatory schools and a university. Simcoe also supported the full endowment of the Church of England. Simcoe had difficulties getting money from England and fought ongoing battles with his superior, Lord Dorchester (Guy Carleton), who was his military commander in Quebec. For his first year in York, he lived with his indefatigable wife, Elizabeth, and their children in a large tent they had bought in London, which had formerly accompanied Captain James Cook on his explorations. Simcoe suffered from poor health and returned to England in 1796. See **CARLTON ST., CASTLE FRANK RD.**

SMALL STREET

Lake Shore Blvd./Queen's Quay   Before Lake Shore Blvd. was built in the 1920s, this street was the southern end of Berkeley St. Once it was separated by the highway, it was renamed Small St. in honour of Major John Small (1746–1831), an early inhabitant of York who was the Clerk of the Executive Council and lived at Berkeley and King for many years. See **BERKELEY ST.**

SORAUREN AVENUE

Lansdowne/Queen   Sorauren was a small town in the Pyrenees where a battle of the Peninsular War was fought against Napoleon. Colonel Walter O'Hara, one of the earliest landowners in Parkdale, named the street after the Spanish village where he had fought under the Duke of Wellington. See **O'HARA AVE.**

SPADINA AVENUE
SPADINA ROAD

Queens Quay to Bloor between Bathurst and University; Bloor to Eglinton between Bathurst and Avenue Rd.   Spadina Ave. was laid out in 1836 by Dr. William Warren Baldwin. He named the street after his house on top of the hill, Spadina (then pronounced "Spadeena"), a word that came from the Native "espadinong," meaning hill. Baldwin built the original Spadina in 1818: a simple two-storey house with a fine view down to the lake. It was situated north of Davenport Rd., just east of where Casa Loma stands today. Baldwin lived there with his family until 1835, when it burned down. He then built a house for himself more conveniently located in the city, but he rebuilt Spadina, and his son Robert Baldwin (1804–58) lived there. Robert died in 1858 and his son sold the house and 80 acres of the estate to James Austin (1813–1897), the president of the Dominion Bank. The Austins transformed Spadina from a simple country home to a magnificent Victorian residence. Austin tore down most of the old house in 1866 and used its original stone foundations to build his new house on a larger scale, with a 42-foot drawing room. His son, Albert Austin, added a billiard room in 1898, and a palm room, terraces and a glassed porte cochere (a glass roof extending from the door to shelter guests arriving by carriage) in 1905. The Austins entertained the fashionable set in Toronto with lavish concerts and receptions. The family lived in Spadina until 1982, when they donated the house to the city as a museum. Today you can visit Spadina House to experience how a prosperous family lived in Victorian Toronto. See **BALDWIN ST., AUSTIN TERRACE.**

CTA SC 244 Item 7338

Looking north from Spadina and Queen in the mid-1920s.

Workers place bricks on Spadina near College in 1899.

SPENCER AVENUE

King/Dufferin Eliza Anne Gywnne inherited the Elm Grove estate from her father, Dr. William Charles Gwynne (1806–75) and subdivided it in 1877. She named this street after one of her father's favourite philosophers, Herbert Spencer (1820–1903). Spencer's work lay in the field of evolutionary theory. A contemporary of Charles Darwin, Spencer believed in the triumph of the individual over society and science over religion. He supported social Darwinism, the school of thought that justified survival of the fittest between competing societies as a natural outcome of evolution. Spencer's most ambitious work was his projected 10-volume opus, *Synthetic Philosophy*. In it he attempted to explain all phenomena in terms of evolutionary progress, covering biology, metaphysics, psychology, sociology and ethics. Between 1862 and 1893 he published 9 of the 10 volumes. Spencer's writing had a great influence on public understanding of the theories of evolution. See **GWYNNE AVE.**

CTA SC 231 Item 1808

STADIUM ROAD

Bathurst/Lake Shore Blvd.   Stadium Rd. runs beside the former site of Maple Leaf Stadium, home of the Toronto Maple Leafs professional baseball team (International League) from 1926 to 1967. Lol Solman, who owned the team at the time, built the 20,000-seat stadium after a dispute with the city. Solman ran the ferries that carried the fans to the games at the stadium at Hanlan's Point Amusement Park on Toronto Island. The city expropriated his ferry company, so Solman built the new stadium at Bathurst and Lake Shore Blvd., where the fans could congregate without crossing the channel. The Maple Leafs ended that first season in 1926 with a bang, winning the Little World Series Championship. They went on to win five more pennants and four Governor's Cup championships at this stadium. They were so successful that the Toronto Maple Leaf Hockey team decided to copy their name in 1931. The colourful Jack Kent Cooke owned the team from 1951 to 1960. He moved on to buy several American sports teams, including the Los Angeles Kings hockey team and the Los Angeles Lakers basketball team, and built the Los Angeles Forum. By all accounts, Maple Leaf Stadium was a fine example of a classic baseball stadium, with tall arched windows, a real dugout, real grass and real dirt. Unfortunately, public interest in baseball flagged and eventually the team went bankrupt and stopped playing in 1967. The stadium was demolished in 1968. See **BASEBALL PLACE, BLUE JAYS WAY, PETER ST.**

STEELES AVENUE

The northern boundary of Toronto: Scarborough/Pickering Townline to Albion Rd., north of Finch.   The Steeles family came to Upper Canada from Yorkshire, England, in 1837 and established themselves as farmers. In 1856 Thomas Steele bought an inn at the northwest corner of Yonge and Steeles. He called it Steele's Hotel, and soon the road it stood on became known as Steele's Ave. The tavern was ideally located for travellers going from York to points north: Richmond Hill, Thornhill and Newmarket. For a while it was called the Green Bush Inn, after a fine balsam tree that grew in front of it. At one point it was a hunt clubhouse and tea room. The business passed on to Thomas' son, John C. Steele, in 1877. John Steele was known later on for his invention to level roads, the Steeles Improved Road Machine, patented in 1896. The building was moved around the corner by a new owner, Thomas Collins, in 1938, and there it stayed until 1970, when it was demolished. Two of the original benches from the inn were rescued and placed in the Black Creek Pioneer Village, located near Jane and Steeles.

STIBBARD AVENUE

Yonge/Eglinton
See **SHELDRAKE BLVD.**

STRACHAN AVENUE

Bathurst/King   Strachan (pronounced "Strawwn") Ave. was originally laid out as a wide street leading up from Wellington to the entrance to Trinity College on Queen St., aligning exactly with the central entrance and tower of the college. Strachan Ave. and the gates remain, but Trinity College was demolished in 1956. The street was named in honour of the founder of Trinity, the first Bishop of Toronto, John Strachan (1778–1867). From 1813, when he lectured the invading American troops and prevented them from further destruction in York, until his death in 1867 on the eve of Confederation, Strachan exerted an enormous influence on the history and development of the city and country. A quarryman's son from Aberdeen, Scotland, Strachan came to Kingston as a young teacher in 1799 and studied divinity in his spare time. Ordained in 1803, he went to Cornwall, where he opened a much-needed boys school. Strachan married very well in 1807 to Ann McGill, the rich widow of a fur trader, Andrew McGill. By 1812 Strachan had been appointed rector at the Church at York, where he made his famous stand against the invading Yankees the following year. The Strachans built a grand house, known as the Palace, that inspired Strachan's visiting brother James to ask, "I hope it's 'a come by honestly, John!" (Robertson, 29). Strachan epitomized the Anglican elite that

TRL T 13802

John Strachan, Toronto's first Anglican Bishop, influenced the city's politics, society and religion for over 50 years.

William Lyon Mackenzie dubbed the Family Compact: rich, Anglican, influential and determined to keep Protestants, Catholics and democracy at bay. He served on the Legislative and Executive councils between 1817 and 1835 and helped to establish Toronto's first university, King's College, in 1827. Strachan worked to maintain Anglican dominance over education and politics, attempting to block all Protestant claims for the Clergy Reserves, a source of great potential wealth in Upper Canada. One-seventh of all public lands had been set aside for building churches and rectories, and the battle for their control was one of the longstanding grievances that led to the Rebellion of 1837. In 1840 Strachan's plans were foiled when the new Governor General, Lord Sydenham, helped to get an act through the Legislative Assembly that provided for the sale of the Clergy Reserves and the division of the profits among the various denominations. Strachan's church became a cathedral in 1839 and Strachan was anointed Bishop. After the Cathedral burned down twice, he set plans in motion to raise money and build a much larger Gothic cathedral with a tower and spire. Begun in 1850, the building opened for worship in 1853 and the tower and spire were finally completed by 1876. Strachan's campaign to build Trinity College began in 1849 when King's College was secularized. Furious at this additional example of weakening Anglican influence, Strachan set out to found a purely Anglican university, travelling to England to raise funds. His efforts were successful, and by 1852 Trinity College opened for students, built on land Strachan bought from Miss Cameron, who owned the Gore Vale property. In the last decade of his life, Strachan created an Anglican synod in his diocese, with the election of new bishops to accommodate the expanding population. He proposed an international convention of Anglican bishops that took place in Lambeth in 1867. He was unable to attend because of poor health and died that same year. Strachan's influence and personality have cast a long shadow over the history of Toronto: St. James' Cathedral, Bishop Strachan School and Trinity College (now part of the University of Toronto) all bear witness to the stubborn energy and determination of this passionate man. See **CARLTON ST., CHURCH ST., COLBORNE ST., GORE VALE AVE., TRINITY CIRCLE.**

John Strachan's home at Front and York was so grand that his brother asked in jest if he had stolen the money to build it.

STRATHGOWAN AVENUE

Lawrence/Yonge Strathgowan Ave. was originally a tree-lined drive leading from Yonge St. to Jesse Ketchum's house, which stood near the corner of St. Hilda's and Strathgowan. Jesse Ketchum (1782–1873), who was to become a very successful businessman and benefactor to the poor, bought this property in the early 1800s. The original lot stretched from Yonge to Bayview between Blythwood and Dawlish. Jesse had come to York from New York State when he was 17 to join his older brother, Seneca Ketchum. They ran a store and farmed, managing to save a considerable amount of money. The story goes that both men were in love with their housekeeper, Ann Love, and they drew lots to decide who should propose to her. Jesse won the draw and Ann accepted his proposal. After they married, Jesse bought this property and built a house there for their growing family. It was a pretty spot, with orchards on both sides of the drive. When Jesse invested in a tannery at Yonge and Queen in 1812, he built another house in town and moved his family there, but he kept the northern property and passed it on to his family when he died. In 1879 the house and 85 acres of the land were sold to John Strathy, a financier involved in the Federal Bank. He named it Strath Gowan, combining his surname with Gowan, his wife's maiden name. The property passed from his family to Nicholas Garland in 1888, and was sold to Wilfrid Dinnick's company for his Lawrence Park subdivision in 1912. See **DINNICK CRESCENT, TEMPERANCE ST.**

This tree-lined drive from Yonge St. to Jesse Ketchum's house eventually became Strathgowan Ave. Circa 1912.

SULLIVAN STREET

Spadina/Queen
See **BALDWIN ST.**

SUMMERHILL AVENUE
SUMMERHILL GARDENS

St. Clair/Yonge   The Summer Hill estate that once occupied 200 acres between Yonge and Bayview had a somewhat chequered early history. The man who built the house, Charles Thompson, suffered financial difficulties and had to convert his drawing room into a public dance hall and open up an amusement park in the Mount Pleasant ravine. The next owner, Larratt William Violett Smith, restored the drawing room to private use and made additions to the house to accommodate his large family. John Howard designed the original building in 1842 for Charles Thompson, who had made his fortune in the transportation business. His stagecoaches on Yonge St. and steamboats on the Great Lakes carried people, mail and goods. However, in 1853 the railway began to make inroads on his business, and he had to sell some of his land and convert another section to a money-making enterprise: an amusement park. Summer Hill Spring Park and Pleasure Grounds offered picnic spots, rides and various entertainments to people venturing up from the city, as well as dancing in his drawing room for the nimble. In 1864 much of his property was subdivided, and in 1866 Larratt William Violett Smith bought the house and the 75 acres remaining in the estate. Smith's successful career as a lawyer and businessman enabled him to finance major additions to the house. He added a number of rooms (bringing the total to 30) and bought a huge 60-by-30-foot Persian rug to cover the floor of the erstwhile dance hall. Orchards and lovely landscaped gardens graced his property. Because he was an ardent bird lover, he banned hunting on his land, which subsequently became a haven for birds of many species. In 1909 the land was subdivided and the house demolished, but an original coach house still can be found on Summerhill Gardens.

TRL T 11521

The drawing room at Summer Hill was once a public dance hall and an amusement park flourished on the grounds. Circa 1900.

SUNLIGHT PARK ROAD

Broadview/Eastern
See **BASEBALL PLACE.**

SUNNYSIDE AVENUE

Queensway/Roncesvalles   Sunnyside Ave. takes its name not from the waterfront amusement park that flourished at the foot of Roncesvalles between 1922 and 1956, but from a house designed by John Howard and sold to John Cheney, who had a business manufacturing stoves. Cheney called his house Sunnyside in homage to Washington Irving (his favourite writer), who had a home called Sunnyside on the Hudson River in New York State. In 1848 Howard bought a strip of land south of Bloor St. between Sunnyside and

Parkside Drive, hoping to subdivide it into lots, build some houses, and then sell them to make a profit. The first house he built was the one Cheney bought in 1853. The house stood on what are now the grounds of St. Joseph's Hospital, overlooking the lake. In those days this was still a wild piece of Canada, with wolves and bears prowling the woods. When Howard laid out the streets in his subdivision, he named Sunnyside Ave. after Cheney's house. He named other streets after the Natives who still used the ancient trail that wound through the property: Indian Road, Indian Grove, Indian Valley Crescent and Indian Trail. It took quite some time for the area to be settled, but by 1888, when it was annexed to Toronto, the whole neighbourhood was known as Sunnyside. The first sign of the coming amusement park in the 20th century was the boardwalk built between 1919 and 1921 along the lake as part of a lakefront development plan. Then came the Sunnyside Bathing Pavilion, the Pavilion Restaurant, the roller coaster, the ferris wheel, the terraced tea garden and the people. They flocked to the amusement park to enjoy all these attractions and eat french fries in paper cones, drink Honey Dew and devour Snowflake Donuts and candy floss. In the 1950s Sunnyside's popularity waned, and when the Gardiner Expressway was built through the area in 1956, the park closed. See **HOWARD PARK AVE.**

Looking northwest along the popular boardwalk at Sunnyside, 1934.

Bathers flocked to the beach at the Sunnyside Pavilion, circa 1924.

SYDENHAM STREET

Parliament/Queen   Lord Sydenham, Charles Edward Poulett Thomson, (1799–1841), was Governor General of British North America for only two years (1839–41), but in that time he managed to profoundly influence the history of Canada. He bullied the legislature into accepting a union between Upper and Lower Canada and introduced a fierce program of anglicization in Quebec that laid the groundwork for ongoing French resentment and resistance. A virulent anti-Reformer, his interference in the electoral process in 1841 ensured that they lost the election. He died in 1841 before he could do any more damage.

TARLTON ROAD

Eglinton/Spadina This street was probably named after a famous British officer who fought in the American Revolution, Colonel Banastre Tarleton (1754–1833). He earned a reputation as a bold war hero because of his relentless pursuit of an American general, Francis Marion. Tarleton hunted Marion throughout much of the war, but Marion (whose nickname was Swamp Fox) constantly eluded him. He and his men concealed themselves in marshes and then executed surprise attacks on the British before fading back into the undergrowth. Tarleton never did catch him, but his tenacity drew admiration from his troops and the United Empire Loyalists that later settled in Upper Canada. His name lost an "e" somewhere along the line.

TECUMSETH PLACE
TECUMSETH STREET

Bathurst/King Tecumseh (1768–1813) was a Shawnee war chief who, like Joseph Brant (Thayendanega), struggled to form a Native alliance to fight against the invasion of the Europeans. Tecumseh tried to save the land the Natives had occupied for generations. After the American Revolution, the Americans moved inexorably west, forcing the Natives into smaller and smaller areas that could not support their customary way of life (hunting, trapping and cultivating land). Tecumseh, whose name means either "shooting star" or "panther crouching in wait," had a brother known as the Prophet, a religious seer. The Prophet urged his people to return to their traditional values and eliminate white influences from their lives. Tecumseth used this growing movement to solidify resistance to the American invasion. He fought in the battle at Fallen Timbers in 1794, in a doomed attempt to save the Ohio Valley. He then moved west to Indiana and spent the next few years trying to rally Native resistance. When the War of 1812 between the British and the Americans broke out, Tecumseh fought with the British at several decisive

TRL T 16600

Tecumseh lived and died courageously struggling to rally Native resistance to European invasion.

battles, in the vain hope that if the British won they would deal more fairly with Native land claims. Tecumseh and his warriors were vital to the British victories at the battle in Detroit in August 1812 (under General Isaac Brock) and at Fort Meigs in May 1813. Then in October 1813 the British fleet was defeated at Put-in-Bay in Ohio, and the British troops on land began a retreat. Tecumseh urged the British to stand and fight, and they finally agreed to make a stand at Moraviantown (now Thamesville). As soon as the Americans attacked, the British broke rank and ran, leaving Tecumseh and 500 of his warriors facing 3,000 American soldiers. Tecumseh was killed. He is remembered for his courage and leadership. See **BRANT ST.**

TEMPERANCE STREET

TRL T 13721

Jesse Ketchum donated huge amounts of his considerable fortune to schools, churches and other worthy causes.

Queen/Yonge   Temperance St. was laid out by Jesse Ketchum (1782–1867) on property that was once part of his tannery at Yonge and Queen. His father had been an alcoholic and his mother died when he was five, leaving 11 children to be cared for in foster homes. As a result, Ketchum became a strong supporter of the Temperance (anti-liquor) movement, and when he moved his tannery business to Buffalo in the late 1830s, he donated some land for a Temperance Hall to be built on Temperance St., with the condition that alcohol would never be served on that street. The hall was later demolished, but Temperance St. remains as a reminder of one of the greatest philanthropists in Toronto's history. Jesse Ketchum lived a life of steady dedication to the public good, supporting schools, churches and the working class. His politics were Reform and his religion was Methodist, both of which placed him in exact opposition to the Anglican elite. Ketchum served as an elected member of the Assembly between 1828 and 1834. He worked closely with William Lyon Mackenzie for reform, inspiring their political enemies to refer to them as "King Jesse" and "King Jesse's jackal." Ketchum drew the line at violence, however, and did not support the armed rebellion of 1837. Ketchum's business interests included his original tannery on Yonge St. and many real estate investments, both in Toronto and Buffalo. He bought the tannery (which occupied the block between Yonge and Bay and Queen and Adelaide) in 1812. The war with the United States gave rise to a sudden demand for boots, so he made a lot of money. It is said that Ketchum gave Muddy York its first sidewalk, on the west side of Yonge between King and Queen, using hemlock tanbark, a byproduct of his tannery. The sidewalk was just the beginning. Over the years Jesse Ketchum's efforts and a great deal of his money and land went towards the construction of churches, temperance halls, schools, libraries and bridges. When he left Toronto in 1845 to live in Buffalo, he gave his employees building lots and helped them find new jobs. His particular interests were temperance, education and religion, and he also founded a bank for the working class in 1830: the Home District Savings Bank. After he moved to Buffalo he continued with his philanthropy in that city. When he died in 1867 the schools there were closed in his honour. See **STRATHGOWAN AVE.**

THORNWOOD ROAD

Yonge/Summerhill
See **PRICE ST.**

TODMORDEN LANE

Pape/Mortimer A small community known as Todmorden Mills grew up around the Helliwell mills in the Don Valley in the 19th century. John Eastwood (1792–1850), who was married to one of the Helliwell daughters, called the mills Todmorden (which means "dead toad" in German!), after his English birthplace. The community was initially made up of the Helliwells and their family and business connections. The Helliwell family came to live in the Don Valley in 1820 when it was still a wilderness where bears, wolves and wildcats were common. The Helliwells were originally from Yorkshire, England, where Thomas Helliwell Sr. (1769–1825) had been a small cotton manufacturer. He acquired 10 acres just south of Pottery Rd. and west of Broadview Ave. and built a brewery and a distillery. He died in 1825. His wife and two of his sons, Thomas and William, took over the business. The Helliwells had an office in Market Square, near their wharf. When Broadview Ave. (then Mill Rd.) was too muddy to use, the Helliwells shipped their beer down the Don River to their wharf in a large dugout canoe. After a fire in 1847 the Helliwells sold their mills. Today Todmorden Mills Heritage Museum occupies the same site and shows how these people lived and worked. There are two restored houses (the Terry House, restored to 1837 and the Helliwell House, restored to 1867), a brewery and a paper mill, now used as an exhibit hall, art gallery and amateur theatre.

The Todmorden site in 1952, with the Helliwell brewery on the left and the Terry house in the background.

TORONTO STREET

Church/King   This street appeared on maps of the town of York as early as 1797, as an extension of Yonge St. below Queen. Over the years it was reduced to its present block-long length. The name Toronto has been the subject of study and conjecture for many years. The commonly accepted meaning, "meeting place," referring to the Native portage at the Humber River, is not accurate. Henry Scadding, the historian who gave us such a detailed picture of the city's history in his 1873 book *Toronto of Old*, perpetuated this interpretation, taken from the Huron word "atonronton," meaning "plenty." This was supposed to refer to "plenty of people" at the portage. Toronto is clearly a word of Native origin, but because the area was occupied by various Native peoples with different languages, the true source of the word is unclear. It first appeared in European records in 1670, on a map that referred to Lake Simcoe as "lac de Taranteau," a French rendition of a Mohawk word "tkaranto," which meant "trees in the water." A Huron word, "ouentaronk," is another possible source. It means "poles that cross." Both words may have referred to a weir built to catch fish in the Narrows between Lake Couchiching and Lake Simcoe. Somehow the name was mistakenly copied down on a map to indicate the portage at the Humber River, and this started to be referred to as "the Toronto portage." The word also referred to the whole area once occupied by the Hurons, between Georgian Bay and Lake Ontario, Lake Huron and Lake Simcoe. The deed that transferred ownership of the land around the original town of York was called the Toronto Purchase. Engineered by Lord Dorchester in 1797, it outlined an area reaching 14 miles east of the Humber River and 28 miles north of the lakeshore, a total of 250,880 acres. Three Mississauga chiefs signed the agreement, selling the area for £1,700 and assorted goods, including cloth, clothes, blankets, fishhooks, farm tools and 96 gallons of rum. See **CARLTON ST., YORK ST.**

CTA SC 231 Item 1667

Automobiles outnumbered horses on Toronto St. north of King in 1915.

TRINITY CIRCLE
TRINITY DRIVE

Dundas/Ossington   These two roads within Trinity-Bellwoods Park commemorate the original Trinity College, one of Bishop Strachan's remarkable achievements. For over a hundred years, from 1852 until 1956, the Trinity College buildings stood on a slight rise overlooking Queen St., with Strachan Ave. leading majestically up to the College grounds. Strachan, an ardent Anglican, started planning an Anglican university when King's College (now the University of Toronto) was secularized in 1849. He bought 20 acres from Miss Cameron, who owned the Gore Vale property, and travelled to England to raise money and support. The first building was completed by 1852; Queen Victoria granted Trinity a Royal Charter, and classes began. A convocation hall and chapel were added in 1877 and 1884, and an east and west wing in 1890 and 1894. The first building, designed by Kivas Tully, was Gothic in character with a central bell tower, loosely modelled on buildings in Oxford and Cambridge. Frank Darling designed the later additions. In 1903 Trinity rejoined the University of Toronto as a federated college, but didn't move to their new building there until 1926. The city nearly tore down the old Trinity College then, but the Kiwanis Club (the same charitable organization that saved Casa Loma) gave it a reprieve by taking over the buildings to use as an athletic club. The rambling structures gradually succumbed to time and neglect: the chapel burned down in 1929 and the other buildings were demolished in 1956. St. Hilda's College, built in 1906, was the only structure to survive. The gates to Trinity College still stand on Queen St., at the entrance to Trinity-Bellwoods Park. See **GORE VALE AVE., STRACHAN AVE.**

TWEEDSMUIR AVENUE

Spadina/St. Clair   John Buchan (1875–1940), Lord Tweedsmuir, served as Canada's Governor General from 1935 until his death in 1940. The Tweed River in Scotland forms part of the border between Scotland and England. Buchan was born in Perth, Scotland. A prolific writer, Buchan published six books before he graduated from Oxford. He is perhaps best known for his thriller *The Thirty-Nine Steps* (1915), which was made into an excellent movie. He also wrote poetry, history and an autobiography, and worked as a literary adviser and director for the publishers Thomas Nelson and Sons. Some of his other occupations during his varied career were a political journalist, a spy during the First World War, a Member of Parliament and a tax lawyer. As Governor General he travelled all over the country, including a trip to the Arctic. He did his best to support the peace efforts instigated by President Roosevelt and Prime Minister Mackenzie King in the years before the outbreak of the Second World War. He appreciated the sense of adventure he found in Canada, which he viewed as a country of vast space and potential. In 1937 he began a tradition that has nurtured Canadian writers ever since: the Governor General's Literary Awards.

TYNDALL AVENUE

Dufferin/King   Eliza Anne Gwynne inherited the Elm Grove estate from her father, Dr. William Charles Gwynne (1806–75) and subdivided it in 1877. She named this street after one of her father's favourite natural philosophers, John Tyndall (1820–93). Tyndall, born in Ireland, was a self-educated man who worked as a surveyor and railway engineer before studying physics. By 1854 he was a professor at the Royal Institute, a prestigious scientific organization in London, England, that supported scientific research. Tyndall's writings and lectures about his research helped to make science popular in the last half of the 19th century. Some of Tyndall's research topics were the movement of glaciers, heat radiation and the acoustic characteristics of the atmosphere. He also discovered something in 1869 called the "Tyndall effect," which involves the scattering of light by colloids. When tiny particles of one substance are mixed with another, but are not completely integrated, they are called colloids. Fog, smoke, homogenized milk and ruby-coloured glass are examples of colloids. Their ability to scatter light (the Tyndall effect) can be illustrated by turning on a flashlight and shining it through a cloud of smoke. The path of the light can be seen. However, if you shine a flashlight through a mixture of salt and water, which forms a true solution, the path of light is invisible. Tyndall had an unfortunate accident with chloral and died from poisoning. See **GWYNNE AVE.**

TYRREL AVENUE

Davenport/Ossington   Joseph Burr Tyrrell (1858–1957) explored large areas of Canada in the west and north between 1881 and 1898, working for the Geological Survey of Canada. He gathered valuable information to supplement the maps made by earlier explorers. Joseph and his brother, James William, made a trip by canoe from Lake Athabasca to Hudson Bay on the Dubawnt River in 1893. James, a civil engineer, wrote a book about their exploits, *Across the Sub-Arctics of Canada* (1897). Among Joseph Tyrrell's many valuable discoveries were dinosaur beds in southern Alberta and coal beds in Alberta and British Columbia. Later Joseph and his brother James went into mining and got quite rich. Joseph Tyrrell also edited the diaries of explorers David Thompson and Samuel Hearne. A mountain and a lake, as well as this street, bear his name, although an "l" got lost along the way for the street.

UNIVERSITY AVENUE

Front to College between Bay and Spadina   King's College was founded in 1827 and granted a large tract of Crown land in the area bounded by Bay and St. George, College St. and Bloor. In 1829 a stately entrance to the future university campus was laid out from Queen to Queen's Park. Initially called College Ave., the street was modelled after elegant drives through French parks and scenic roadways in Oxford and Cambridge (Queen's Road and Backs drives). The avenue formed a park cut off from the rest of the city. At Queen St. John Howard built a gatehouse, and another gatehouse marked the entrance at what is now College and Yonge. Commercial traffic was stopped at the gates. Lined with pink flowering chestnuts, boulevards and walkways, the 120-foot-wide street became a favourite spot for promenades. Originally there were two roadways divided by a median: the west side was called College Ave. and the east side was called Park Lane, after the elegant street in London that runs beside Hyde Park. The growing city outside the gates and fences that isolated College Ave. eventually forced an end to its private, exclusive nature, and in 1859 the fences came down and traffic was allowed to cross the street. At this point it was renamed University to avoid confusion with College St. See **CARLTON ST.**

John Howard designed the Queen St. entrance gates to College Ave. (now University). Circa 1868.

University Ave. was originally an elegant drive cut off from all east-west traffic. Circa 1897.

VAN HORNE AVENUE

W.A. Cooper NAC PA 182603

William Van Horne created the Canadian transcontinental railway, the CP hotels and the Empress steamships.

Finch/Leslie   William Cornelius Van Horne (1843–1915) began his long and successful career in railways at the age of 14 as a telegrapher for the Illinois Central Railroad. He worked for American railroad companies for the next 25 years and then moved to Canada to take on the position of general manager of the Canadian Pacific Railway in 1882. Van Horne brought his extraordinary energy and organizational skills to bear on the building of the Canadian transcontinental railway. One of the conditions of bringing British Columbia into Confederation in 1871 was the construction of this railway. Work began in 1880, and once Van Horne took over, everything moved more quickly and more efficiently. By August 1883 he had managed to complete the line across the prairies between Winnipeg and Calgary. Two years later the railroad was finished all the way to Fort Moody, British Columbia. The first transcontinental train ran from Montreal to Port Moody during the summer of 1886. Van Horne received much of the credit for completing the massive project so quickly. He was made president of Canadian Pacific in 1888 and kept the wheels turning: the Empress steamships and the CP hotels were two of his larger projects. The steamships were built to cross the Pacific Ocean, carrying mail, passengers and freight. Because of their speed and luxurious appointments, they stimulated trade and tourism between the Orient and Canada. In 1894 he was given a knighthood, and in 1899 he retired. The construction of the transcontinental railway in Canada played a vital role in the development of this country, and Van Horne's name will always be associated with that great achievement.

VICTORIA STREET

King/Yonge
See **QUEEN ST.**

WALKER AVENUE

St. Clair/Yonge   This street once marked the northern boundary of the village of Yorkville. It was named after the Walker factory, which stood there from the mid-19th century until the 1920s. John Walker, a wheelwright, ran the factory, which made wheels, brickmakers' supplies and the large wooden tanks that were placed in attics and filled with water in case of fire. John's father, Walter Walker, came to Canada from England in 1832 and established a wagon-making shop on Bloor St. He soon moved up to where Walker St. is today. Walter and another one of his sons, Albert Woodland Walker, established a store that sold hardware supplies. This store eventually became known as North Toronto Hardware, a business that thrived well into the 20th century, operated by Walker descendants.

WALMER ROAD

Bloor/Spadina   When Robert Baldwin, the grandson of Dr. William Warren Baldwin, sold some of the Spadina estate for development in 1873, he named Walmer Rd. after the English birthplace of his son. Unlike most of the streets in Toronto, which were laid out on the grid system, Walmer Rd. was designed to curve: an elegant street intended to attract wealthy people to build there. Walmer, Kent, is a town northeast of Dover on the English Channel. Henry VIII (b. 1491, r. 1509–1547) originally built Walmer Castle as a fortification for coastal defence. In 1730 it was converted into an official residence for the Lord Warden of the Cinque Ports. These were the five ports on the English Channel (Hastings, Sandwich, Dover, Romney, Hythe) given special privileges by Edward I (1239–1307) for defending the coast. One of the most famous Lord Wardens was the Duke of Wellington, who lived in Walmer Castle from 1829 until his death in 1852. Another was Winston Churchill. The Queen Mother is the present Lord Warden, but she seldom stays at Walmer Castle. It is a now a pleasant country house, open to visitors and surrounded by lovely gardens. The moat is used for a walking path around the castle. See **BALDWIN ST., O'HARA AVE., RAGLAN AVE., ROBERT ST., SPADINA AVE., WELLESLEY ST.**

Walmer Rd. north of Davenport in 1913, with Casa Loma's stables and carriage house in the background.

CTA SC 231 Item 1778

WAVERLY ROAD

Queen/Woodbine   *Waverley* (1814) was a historical novel by Walter Scott (1771–1832), one of the most popular English writers of his time. A poet and novelist, Scott was more than anything an excellent storyteller. A hard worker with a prodigious output, Scott wrote at a feverish pitch, especially in the last few years of his life. His punishing work schedule certainly contributed to his final illness and death. Often referred to as the "Father of the Historical Novel," Scott wrote about romantic subjects from the past, often set in his native Scotland, and he didn't let facts get in the way of the story. For much of his working life he held the post of sheriff-deputy, which his training as a lawyer equipped him to fulfil. This provided him with some income and lots of free time to write. He started with poetry and then moved on to novels. After the success of the first *Waverley* novel, he wrote a series of others. He published them anonymously and didn't admit he had written them until 1827. He ran into terrible problems with debt when the publishing company he was involved with collapsed, and the frantic writing schedule of his last years was a result of his determination to pay off the massive amount owing. His royalties finally paid it off 15 years after his death. Scott was made a baronet in 1820. A dashing, romantic figure who loved to gallop over the fields while composing poetry, Scott spent much of his time in his country house in Scotland with his wife and family. He loved to entertain, and enjoyed buying land and planting it with trees. The British government sent him on a cruise to the Mediterranean in 1931 in the hope that his health would improve, but it deteriorated, and he came home to die. Some of his better known books are *The Lady of the Lake* (1810), *The Bride of Lammermoor* (1819), *Ivanhoe* (1819) and *Kenilworth* (1821). The street name lost an "e" somewhere along the line.

WELLESLEY AVENUE
WELLESLEY COTTAGES
WELLESLEY LANE
WELLESLEY PLACE
WELLESLEY STREET

Carlton/Parliament; Carlton/Sherbourne; Carlton/Yonge   Arthur Wellesley (1769–1852), the 1st Duke of Wellington, is best known for his defeat of Napoleon at the battle of Waterloo in 1815. Before that he had an illustrious military career, including several decisive campaigns in India between 1796 and 1805, while his brother, Richard Wellesley, served as Governor General of that country. During the Peninsular War against Napoleon (1809–13), Wellesley commanded the combined forces of British, Portuguese and Spanish armies to fight Napoleon's army. He finally drove the French out and went home, where he was created the Duke of Wellington. Two years later he had to return to the battlefield to defeat Napoleon once more, at Waterloo. After this battle, Wellesley gradually became involved in politics as a Conservative and held various positions. He was Prime Minister from 1828 to 1830. His tenure didn't go well. Some of his policies were so unpopular that a mob attacked his house. In 1846 he retired from politics. One of the final honours awarded to him was his burial in St. Paul's Cathedral. See **O'HARA AVE., RAGLAN AVE., RONCESVALLES AVE., WALMER RD.**

WELLINGTON STREET

King/Yonge
See **WELLESLEY ST.**

The Toronto Exchange on the north side of Wellington St. east of Yonge, 1856.

WELLS HILL AVENUE
WELLS STREET

Bathurst/St. Clair; Bathurst/Dupont
See **DAVENPORT RD.**

WEST LODGE AVENUE

Lansdowne/Queen
See **O'HARA AVE.**

WESTMORELAND AVENUE

Bloor/Dovercourt   Whether this street was named after Westmorland County in northern England (with an extra "e") or after a family who lived in the area is unclear. Westmorland joined with Cumberland and parts of Lancashire to form the new county of Cumbria in 1974. The picturesque Lake District is located in Westmorland. Lake Windermere, the biggest lake in England (six square miles), lies on the west border. The poet laureate William Wordsworth (1770–1850) lived in the village of Grasmere on Lake Grasmere. A high, mountainous country ideal for raising sheep and cattle, its location near the Scottish border resulted in a number of raids, invasions and battles in its early history. Now the dramatic scenery of the Lake District, the inspiration for poets and novelists for centuries, draws tourists from all over the world. See **CUMBERLAND ST.**

WHITNEY AVENUE

Mount Pleasant/St. Clair   This street was named in 1908 by the developers' lawyer, Roderick James MacLennan, when the street was laid out. He named it after the Premier of Ontario at that time, Sir James Pliny Whitney (1843–1914). Whitney, a blacksmith's son from Williamsburg who went to school at the Cornwall Grammar School, was called to the bar in 1876. In 1888 he won a seat in the Dundas riding for the Conservatives and entered a life of politics. Eight years later he was the leader of the party, with his work cut out for him. His leadership brought his dispirited party into the 20th century with renewed policies, organization and a sense of mission that culminated in their 1905 defeat of the longstanding Liberal government, which had been in power for 33 years. As Premier, Whitney set about to make reforms. Under his government Ontario's hydroelectric service became a publicly owned company, the University of Toronto's financial base was assured, and workmen's compensation legislation was introduced. However, a controversial issue in the form of the Ontario Schools Question raised its ugly head and Whitney's handling of it was less than satisfactory, stirring up a national unity crisis. In 1912 his government, under pressure from Protestants and English-speaking Catholics, passed Regulation 17, which curtailed French-language instruction for French-speaking children to the first two years of elementary school. In 1913 this instruction was limited further to one hour per day. Francophones in Ontario and Quebec were outraged, and this issue added fuel to the conscription crisis in Quebec during the First World War. Regulation 17 remained an issue (it proved impossible to enforce) until 1927, when a compromise was reached whereby each school's situation was evaluated separately. See **HIGHLAND AVE.**

WIDMER STREET

King/Spadina   York General Hospital, founded in 1818, once stood near the corner of King and Front streets. After the Legislative buildings burned down in 1824, the Assembly took over the hospital for their meeting place until the new buildings were ready in 1829. When the hospital was demolished and the property divided, Widmer St. was laid out and named after one of its founders, Dr. Christopher Widmer (1780–1858). The accounts of Widmer's life and character paint a fascinating picture of a man with many talents. As a young man, Widmer trained as a doctor and then joined the army, where he became an army surgeon. He was in the army from 1804 until 1817, spending six of those years in the Iberian Peninsula during the Peninsular Wars against Napoleon. His army experiences are said to have formed certain aspects of his character: his stern, gruff manner, upright carriage and propensity for colourful swearing. A consummate ladies' man, he lived childless with his first wife for thirty years, and after she died, married his mistress and had four children with her. His first wife, Emily Sarah Bignell, came from a rich family, while his second wife, Hannah, was from a much lower stratum of society. Widmer came to Canada with the army in 1814. Three years later he retired from the army and set up a medical practice in York. As one of the few qualified doctors in the town, he was soon involved in creating the hospital and trying to improve medical services and medical education. One of the first members of the Medical Board of Upper Canada, Widmer served on the commission to build the first lunatic asylum and spent years struggling to establish a medical school connected with the university, King's College. As an outstanding public figure in a relatively small community, and a close friend of William Warren Baldwin, another early doctor in York, and his son Robert, who became a leading figure in Reform politics, Widmer was inevitably drawn into political life. Up to the eve of the Rebellion of 1837, Widmer was a Conservative. Then he switched to Reform, perhaps partially in response to the outrageous behaviour of Lieutenant Governor Sir Francis Bond Head. Widmer did not support armed insurrection, however, and during the Rebellion he was in charge of the army's medical department. Widmer also served as a justice of the peace for 20 years and had various business interests, including a directorship at the Bank of Canada. His medical ability was well respected; he kept up-to-date with the latest developments and performed surgery well into his 70s with skill and expertise. An adept horseman, at the age of 61 he rode from Toronto to Kingston without a break to tend to Lord Sydenham on his deathbed. Widmer was honoured by the Royal College of Surgeons in London, England, in 1844, when they elected him a fellow of that institution. In 1858, while visiting the grave of his son, who had died a year before, Widmer was struck down by a seizure from which he never recovered. See **BALDWIN ST., PARLIAMENT ST., REES ST., WELLESLEY ST.**

WILLCOCKS STREET

Harbord/Spadina
See **BALDWIN ST.**

WILLOWBANK BOULEVARD

Avenue Rd./Eglinton   Willowbank was the name of a house built by John J. Gartshore in the 1890s. It still stands today, at the corner of Oriole Parkway and Burnaby Blvd. Gartshore inherited the property and another house, called the Willows, from his former employer, James Lesslie, who had bought the Willows from James Hervey Price of Castlefield. Price in turn had bought the house from John Montgomery in 1843. The Willows was the famous house that Montgomery and his family were in the process of moving into when the

Rebellion broke out in 1837. Lesslie was a good friend of William Lyon Mackenzie: they came to Canada together in the 1820s from Dundee, Scotland. Lesslie went into the printing business and eventually owned a newspaper. Over the years, Lesslie worked steadily through his pro-Reform articles to sway public opinion in favour of responsible government. Lesslie kept peacocks and other livestock on his farm and planted extensive orchards, thought to be the inspiration for the naming of the nearby Orchard View Blvd. When he died in 1885, he divided his property between his widow, Jacqueline, and Gartshore, who had managed his estate and farm. Jacqueline willed her part of the estate to Gartshore, who built a larger house and called it Willowbanks. An active member of the Eglinton Presbyterian Church, he used the old Willows house for accommodation for visiting and retired missionaries. In 1910, with the developing subdivision encroaching the farm, Gartshore sold the property. The house became the club house for the Eglinton branch of the Toronto Hunt Club, with enlarged dining facilities and kitchens, and huge stables for 140 horses. In 1939 the RCAF took it over to use as a training school. The house is now owned by the Metropolitan Toronto School Board. See **CASTLEFIELD AVE., MONTGOMERY AVE.**

Horse-drawn carts line up along a Toronto street outside the East End City Stables in 1911.

WINCHESTER STREET

Carlton/Parliament   Winchester is a county town in Hampshire, England, about 62 miles southwest of London, which was the centre of the woollen trade in the 14th century. In ancient times Winchester was the capital of Wessex, the kingdom of the West Saxons, founded in 519. In those days the Saxons were divided into four kingdoms in Britain, and Wessex was the strongest. Alfred the Great (848–99) is probably the most famous King of Wessex. He fought against the invading Danes and encouraged education among his people, translating books from Latin to English. Winchester Cathedral, built between 1070 and 1098, is dedicated to Saint Swithin, an early bishop of Winchester who died in 862. Saint Swithin is the source of a superstition particularly suited to the English climate: in 971, after he was made a saint, they attempted to move his body to the Cathedral to be buried there. But extreme rain fell for 40 days and they had to wait until all the storms were over. Ever since, if it rains on St. Swithin's Day (July 15), people believe that it will rain every day for the next forty days. Winchester Cathedral, whose great length (556 feet) makes it the longest cathedral in Europe, is the burial place of Jane Austen.

WINDSOR AVENUE
WINDSOR ROAD
WINDSOR STREET

Queen/Victoria Park; Dixon/Kipling; Evans/Royal York Road; Front/Spadina
These streets all take their names from either the House of Windsor, which is the British Royal Family's surname, or their home at Windsor Castle, located in the small town of Windsor just 22 miles west of London. Because of the strong anti-German feelings aroused in Britain during the First World War, King George V (b. 1865, r. 1910–36) changed the family name from Saxe-Coburg-Gotha to the more English-sounding Windsor. The site of Windsor Castle was chosen as a royal residence by William the Conqueror (b. 1027, r. 1066–87) because its position on a chalk cliff was easy to defend and it was close to Windsor Forest, an excellent hunting ground. Windsor Castle, the

largest castle in the world that people actually live in, was built in stages by various monarchs. William the Conqueror started with a wooden stockade in 1070, Henry II built the stone Round Tower castle in 1180, and over the centuries it gradually grew from a fort into the palace it is today. In 1992 a fire started in the Private Chapel when a spotlight ignited a curtain. It raged for 15 hours, destroying one-fifth of the Castle, including 9 of the principal rooms and 100 other rooms. It took 250 firefighters and one-and-a-half million gallons of water to extinguish the fire. A huge restoration project then began, and five years and 37 million pounds later it was completed. The Queen raised some of the money by allowing paying visitors into Buckingham Palace.

CTA SC 266 Item 1881

Horses wait patiently as ice is delivered house-to-house in January, 1924.

WITHROW AVENUE

Broadview/Gerrard   John Jacob Withrow (1833–1900) is remembered primarily for his key role in the creation of the Toronto Industrial Exhibition in 1879, which became the Canadian National Exhibition in 1912. However, he was involved in numerous other ventures, including the development of a subdivision in 1886 east of Broadview, centred around Withrow Ave. Withrow formed a building company with John Hillock in 1865, constructing buildings and selling lumber, windows and doors. Despite his forays into politics (election as an alderman in 1873 and two unsuccessful attempts at the office of mayor) and his involvement in various business concerns, he remained a builder for most of his life. One of his biggest projects was the carpentry work on Massey Hall in the 1880s. As chairman of the Board of Trustees that operated Massey Hall, he was the only trustee who was not a member of the Massey family. A staunch Methodist, Withrow lent his support to charitable projects, such as the building of an orphanage in 1883 on Hanlan's Point, called the Lakeside Home for Little Children. With other Methodist businessmen he founded a company in the early 1880s to encourage settlement in Saskatchewan: the Saskatchewan Land and Homestead Company. But his contribution to the CNE remains his crowning achievement to the millions of people who have enjoyed the end-of-the-summer ritual of "going to the Ex." Agricultural exhibitions and fairs have been a part of our history since the early settlement of Upper Canada. An annual provincial exhibition began in 1846, held at different towns each year. Because Toronto drew on the largest population, the fair was always very successful here and in 1878 the exhibition committee, led by Withrow, planned to make it permanent. The Provincial Fair Association had no such intention, having chosen Ottawa as their location for 1879. Withrow and his committee formed the Industrial Exhibition Association and held their own fair the following summer. It was a great success and is still going strong over 120 years later. Withrow served as president of the Exhibition from 1879 until 1900. The CNE has transformed from a chiefly agricultural exhibition to a consumer-oriented exhibition and amusement park. It owes its existence to the enthusiasm and drive of John Jacob Withrow. See **MASSEY ST.**

WOLSELEY STREET

Bathurst/Queen   Lord Garnet Joseph Wolseley (1833–1913) was a distinguished British soldier whose army career led him all over the world. He served in India, South Africa, Egypt, China, the Crimea and Canada. He rose through the ranks to the position of Commander-in-Chief of the British Army, which he held between 1895 and 1900. His position in Canada, first as the Assistant Quartermaster General in 1861 and then as the Deputy Quartermaster General in 1865, led to his command of the troops sent to suppress the Red River Rebellion led by Louis Riel in 1870. This street was named after him shortly after this expedition. Wolseley also wrote books; his most well known publication was an account of his life in the army called *The Story of a Soldier's Life* (1903). Another book he wrote was a practical guide that was widely read in the army and ran into several editions: *Soldiers' Pocket Book for Field Service* (1869).

WOOD STREET

Carlton/Yonge
See **ALEXANDER ST.**

WOODLAWN AVENUE

St. Clair/Yonge   Woodlawn Ave. was originally the driveway that led from Yonge St. to Woodlawn, a lovely house designed by the architect John Howard (who later donated High Park to the city) in 1840 for William Hume Blake (1809–70). The house still survives today in a much smaller form, as 35 Woodlawn Ave. West. It has been lived in by the same family since the 1920s and carefully restored by them. The house Howard designed for Blake was a two-storey Regency villa with a ballroom. Blake and his wife Catherine lived at Woodlawn for three years and then sold it to his law partner, Joseph Curran

Morrison (1816–85) in 1844. Blake later built Humewood as his country house. Morrison married Elizabeth Bloore, who was the daughter of Joseph Bloore, for whom Bloor St. was named. They added a huge 40-by-50-foot greenhouse and conservatory to the house. In 1863 Morrison became a judge and chancellor of the University of Toronto. He and his wife used the gracious setting of Woodlawn to entertain their friends with parties and balls. They held an annual champagne breakfast every July 1. After Morrison died in 1885 his estate was subdivided for housing developments and part of the house was demolished. But in 1895 his heir, Angus Morrison, built a new wing to accommodate a new kitchen and bedrooms. The house that survives today still retains the original thick pine floors, inner shutters and walnut woodwork. See **BLOOR ST., HOWARD PARK AVE., HUMEWOOD DR.**

W O O D S W O R T H   R O A D

Leslie/York Mills   From preaching in Manitoba as a Methodist circuit rider, to working as a longshoreman on the Vancouver docks, to being arrested during the Winnipeg General Strike, and finally to being elected to Parliament representing a new socialist party, James Shaver Woodsworth (1874–1942) lived his very public life according to his conscience. He moved to Manitoba from Ontario with his family when he was a child and soon followed his father into the ministry in the Methodist Church. However, he had grave misgivings about the church's emphasis on personal salvation in light of the desperate social conditions in England and Canada. Woodsworth developed into an ardent democratic socialist and a pacifist. His opposition to conscription during the First World War cost him a government research job in 1917, and the following year he quit the ministry in response to the Methodists' support of the war. This is when he ended up in Vancouver working as a longshoreman to support his family. He was arrested during the Winnipeg General Strike in 1919 after writing editorials denouncing the government's brutal response to the strikers. The publicity earned him a certain amount of public support that helped him win the election two years later that sent him to Ottawa. There Woodsworth learned how to use parliamentary procedure to achieve some of his goals. He used his position as a member of the opposition to hound the government unmercifully on policies he objected to, and in the process helped to establish the working principles of a multiparty parliamentary system. He managed to persuade Prime Minister Mackenzie King to introduce an old-age pension plan in 1927 by trading the somewhat insecure King two votes. This was the first step towards establishing a social security system in Canada. In 1933 a federal socialist party was born with Woodsworth as its leader: the Co-operative Commonwealth Federation (CCF), which later became the New Democratic Party. In the late 1930s, with the imminent outbreak of another world war, Woodsworth once more acted according to his ideals: as a pacifist he opposed war no matter what the provocation. When war was declared he was the only Member of Parliament who declared his opposition in the legislature. He died as the result of a stroke in 1942. Woodsworth College at the University of Toronto was named in his honour.

WYCHWOOD AVENUE
WYCHWOOD PARK

Bathurst/Davenport   Wychwood Park, originally envisioned as an artist's colony by the two men who bought the property in the 1870s, remains a charming enclave in the heart of the city. The original house, Wychwood, still stands there. Marmaduke Matthews (1837–1913) built it in 1874 and named it after Wychwood Forest in Oxfordshire, near where he grew up. He and his friend Alexander Jardine, who owned the Pure Gold Baking Powder Company, bought more property in 1877 and Jardine built a house slightly to the west of Wychwood called Braemore. Braemore Gardens owes its name to Jardine's house. The two friends now owned all the land from Davenport up to St. Clair between Bathurst and Christie, and they hoped to establish an artist's colony there. The first step towards this goal was taken in 1888 when they subdivided the land into 18 large lots, 17 for building and one to remain as a park. In 1891 they subdivided it again, into 38 smaller lots. They set up a system of trusteeship so that the residents could control the development of the area. Taddle Creek was dammed to form a pond (much larger than the one that remains today) where residents could skate in winter and swim in summer. Other artists gradually moved in and built houses. Many were designed in the Cottage Style popular at the time, by the architect Eden Smith, who himself became one of Wychwood Park's residents. The style was reminiscent of English cottages: swooping rooflines, exposed timbers, leaded-glass windows and huge fireplaces. Wychwood Park retains some of the atmosphere of an English village. It has been administered by a corporation since 1907, even though it was annexed by the city of Toronto in 1909. A board of trustees makes most of the decisions that affect the residents. Matthews first came to Toronto in 1860 and four years later left in a hurry when he eloped with Cyrilda Barnard to New York. But they returned in 1869 with several children and in 1873 bought the Wychwood property. Matthews held the position of official artist for the Canadian Pacific Railway in the 1880s and 1890s, and in that capacity painted many western landscapes. He lived with his large family at Wychwood until his death in 1913, and then his daughter Alice lived there until 1960. Among Wychwood Park's more famous residents was the internationally renowned University of Toronto professor and media guru, Marshall McLuhan. See **VAN HORNE AVE.**

The lovely Wychwood ravine in 1907.

YONGE STREET

Queen's Quay to Steeles between Bayview and Bathurst   Toronto's main street was also its first street. When Governor Simcoe arrived in what was to be the town of York in 1793, one of his chief concerns was to establish a military presence to defend the country in the event of an American invasion, which he considered inevitable. He wanted to build a military road between the harbour at York and Lake Simcoe, which was part of the waterway system that led to Georgian Bay and the Upper Great Lakes. The road would provide a route to York for British troops stationed at military posts in the Upper Great Lakes. In February 1794 the first survey and marking of the road was begun by the Deputy Surveyor, Augustus Jones (1758–1837), and a detachment of the Queen's Rangers. To cut a road through the dense bush required skill and a great deal of hard labour. Jones preferred to work in the dead of winter, when the leafless trees made it easier to survey the lie of the land. The Rangers cut a rough path 20 feet wide and laid out 200-acre lots on each side of the road. They got to Thornhill by August, when increasing tensions with the Americans called a temporary halt to the building of the road because the Rangers were needed at the Niagara border. Another group of men led by William von Berczy worked on a stretch between Thornhill and Langstaff, but severe weather conditions and sickness prevented them from advancing any farther. In January 1796 the Rangers and Augustus Jones returned to complete the job, and in 43 days they reached Lake Simcoe, at the spot that later became Gwillimbury. Simcoe named Yonge St. after his old friend, Sir George Yonge (1731–1812), who as the Secretary of War in 1791 had signed the document designating the Queen's Rangers as a regiment to protect the new province. Yonge never visited Canada, but he had a long association with Simcoe as the Member of Parliament for Honiton, the location of Simcoe's country estate in England. After his term as Secretary of War, Yonge was appointed Master of the Mint and then Governor of the Cape of Good Hope. He had a lifetime interest in roads and their construction from Roman times, so it is perhaps fitting that his name graces Yonge St. From Queen's Quay to Rainy River, where Yonge St., in its continuation as Highway 11, finally ends, it measures 1,178.3 miles, which makes it the longest street in the world, earning a mention in the *Guiness Book of World Records*. See **CASTLE FRANK RD., SIMCOE ST.**

Spring crowds throng the sidewalks at Queen and Yonge (looking north) in April, 1938.

YORK STREET

King/University   When Simcoe founded the town of York in 1793, he was in the habit of stoutly changing every name with a Native, French or American flavour to a plain, loyal English name. This was part of his campaign to anglicize Upper Canada (which had been chiefly inhabited by Natives and the French until this time.) So Niagara became Newark, Lac La Claie (Fence Lake) became Lake Simcoe, and Toronto became York. This was in honour of the Duke of York, Frederick Augustus (1763–1827), who had just won a victory in Flanders in the French Revolutionary Wars. York was the second son of George III, with a career in the army that saw him rise from Colonel at the age of 17 to Commander-in-Chief at 35. He had a moderate success in

Flanders, but when he returned to Europe in 1799 as Commander-in-Chief he failed miserably. Back in England he showed some talent at carrying out reforms within the army, but a scandal with a woman forced him to retire from the army in 1809. When Simcoe named the town York, the Duke was at the peak of his success and popularity, but his fortunes soon fell. Over the years the name York lost its lustre, and the ignominy of its nicknames, Muddy York and Little York (as compared with New York), gave rise to a movement to change the name back to Toronto. This was accomplished when it was incorporated as a city in 1834. There has been some debate as to whether York St. was named after the Duke of York, or if it came by its name because it was the road to York. Travellers coming to the city along Dundas Rd. and then Lot St. (now Queen) would turn off here if they were going to York, rather than continuing along Lot past the town to Kingston Road. See **SIMCOE ST.**, **TORONTO ST.**

Looking north on York St. to Osgoode Hall in 1857.

CTA SC 498 Item 16

Bibliography

Adam, G. Mercer. *Toronto, Old and New: A Memorial Volume – Historical, Descriptive and Pictorial*. 1891. Facsimile edition. Coles Publishing Company. Toronto: 1974.

Armstrong, Frederick H. *A City in the Making: Progress, People and Perils in Victorian Toronto*. Dundurn Press. Toronto: 1988.

Armstrong, Frederick H. *Toronto: The Place of Meeting*. Windsor Publications. Toronto: 1983.

Arthur, Eric. *No Mean City*. 3rd ed. University of Toronto Press. Toronto: 1986.

Benson, Eugene, and L.W. Conolly, eds. *The Oxford Companion to Canadian Theatre*. Oxford University Press. Toronto: 1989.

Berchem, F.R. *The Yonge Street Story, 1793–1860: An Account from Letters, Diaries and Newspapers*. McGraw-Hill Ryerson. Toronto: 1977.

Bercuson, David J., and J.L. Granatstein. *The Collins Dictionary of Canadian History, 1867 to the Present*. Collins. Toronto: 1988.

Blazing a Road to Grandeur: North York's Yonge Street Communities. City of North York Parks and Recreation Department, 1996.

Bonis, Robert R. *A History of Scarborough*. Scarborough Public Library. Scarborough, Ontario: 1965.

Boylen, John Chancellor. *York Township: An Historical Summary*, 1850–1954. Municipal Corporation of the Township of York and the Board of Education of the Township of York. Toronto: 1954.

Brown, Sheila Jean, ed. *Researching Yonge Street*. Ontario Genealogical Society, Toronto Branch. Toronto: 1996.

Byers, Nancy, and Barbara Myrvold. *St. Clair West in Pictures: A History of the Communities of Carlton, Davenport, Earlscourt, and Oakwood*. Local History Handbook No. 8. Toronto Public Library. Toronto: 1997.

Campbell, Mary, and Barbara Myrvold. *The Beach in Pictures, 1793–1932*. Local History Handbook No. 6. Toronto Public Library. Toronto: 1988.

Campbell, Mary, and Barbara Myrvold. *Historical Walking Tour of Kew Beach*. Toronto Public Library. Toronto: 1995.

The Canadian Encyclopedia. Edited by James H. Marsh. Hurtig Publishers. Edmonton: 1985.

The Canadian Encyclopedia 1999 World Edition. 2 CD ROMs. McClelland & Stewart. Toronto: 1998.

Careless, J.M.S. *Toronto to 1918: An Illustrated History*. James Lorimer & Company and National Museum of Man. Toronto: 1984.

Compton's Encyclopedia 1999. The Learning Company. Novato, California: 1998.

Dendy, William. *Lost Toronto*. 2nd ed. McClelland & Stewart. Toronto: 1983.

Dendy, William, and William Kilbourn. *Toronto Observed: Its Architecture, Patrons, and History*. Oxford University Press. Toronto: 1986.

Dictionary of Canadian Biography. 12 volumes. Frances G. Halpenny, ed. University of Toronto Press. Toronto: 1966–1990.

Drabble, Margaret, ed. *The Oxford Companion to English Literature*. 5th ed. Oxford University Press. London: 1985.

Encyclopaedia Britannica. William Benton. Chicago: 1960.

Encyclopaedia Britannica. 11th ed. Cambridge University Press. Cambridge: 1910.

Filey, Mike. *Discover and Explore Toronto's Waterfront: A Walker's Jogger's Cyclist's Boater's Guide to Toronto's Lakeside Sites and History*. Dundurn Press. Toronto: 1998.

Filey, Mike. *More Toronto Sketches: "The Way We Were."* Dundurn Press. Toronto: 1993.

Filey, Mike. *Mount Pleasant Cemetery: An Illustrated Guide*. 2nd ed. Dundurn Press. Toronto: 1999.

Filey, Mike. *Toronto Flashbacks 1*. Firefly Books. Toronto: 1989.

Filey, Mike. *Toronto Flashbacks 2*. Firefly Books. Toronto: 1989.

Filey, Mike. *Toronto Sketches 3. "The Way We Were."* Dundurn Press. Toronto: 1994

Filey, Mike. *Toronto Sketches 4: "The Way We Were."* Dundurn Press. Toronto: 1995.

Filey, Mike. *Toronto Sketches 5: "The Way We Were."* Dundurn Press. Toronto: 1997.

Filey, Mike. *The TTC Story: The First Seventy-Five Years*. Dundurn Press. Toronto: 1996.

Filey, Mike, and Victor Russell. *From Horse Power to Horsepower: Toronto: 1890–1930.* Dundurn Press. Toronto: 1993.

Fraser, Antonia, ed. *The Lives of the Kings and Queens of England*. Alfred A. Knopf. New York: 1975.

Fulford, Robert. *Accidental City: The Transformation of Toronto*. Macfarlane, Walter & Ross. Toronto: 1995.

Goad, Charles Edward. *The Mappings of Victorian Toronto*. Paget Press. Toronto: 1984.

Guthrie, Ann. *Don Valley Legacy: A Pioneer History*. Boston Mills Press. Erin, Ontario: 1986.

Hampshire County Council. "Winchester Cathedral." <hants.gov.uk/cgi-bin/fx.phrase?DB=rest_hantsweb>

History of Toronto and County of York, Ontario. C. Blackett Robinson. Toronto: 1885.

Hopkins, Jeanne. *The Henry Farm, Oriole: An Early Settlement of North York*. Henry Farm Community Interest Association. Willowdale: 1987.

Hopkins, Jeanne. "Signpost" and "Looking Back." Series of articles published in *Post* newspapers (*Bayview Post, North Toronto Post, Thornhill Post, Village Post*) and *Real Estate News*. 1991–99.

Hopkins, Jeanne. *York Mills Heights: Looking Back*. York Mills Heights Association. 1998.

Hurwitz, Howard L. *An Encyclopedic Dictionary of American History*. Washington Square Press. New York: 1968.

Hutcheson, Stephanie. *Yorkville in Pictures, 1853 to 1883*. Local History Handbook No. 2. Toronto Public Libraries. Toronto: 1978.

Jarvis, Mary Hoskin. *Historical Street Names of Toronto*. Canada: 1931–34.

Johnson, Norah. *The Irish in Toronto's Old Ward 5*. Community History Project, Spadina Road Library. Toronto: 1992.

Jones, Donald. *Fifty Tales of Toronto*. University of Toronto Press. Toronto: 1994.

Kelly, Colleen. *Cabbagetown in Pictures*. Local History Handbook No. 4. Toronto Public Library. Toronto: 1984.

Kilbourn, William. *Toronto Remembered: A Celebration of the City*. Stoddart Publishing. Toronto: 1984.

Kinsella, Joan C. *Historical Walking Tour of Deer Park*. Toronto Public Library. Toronto: 1996.

Langton, Anne. *A Gentlewoman in Upper Canada: The Journal of Anne Langton*. Edited by Hugh Hornby Langton. Clarke Irwin. Toronto: 1950.

Langton, John. *Early Days in Upper Canada: Letters of John Langton from the Backwoods of Upper Canada*. Edited by William A. Langton. Macmillan. Toronto: 1926.

Laycock, Margaret, and Barbara Myrvold. *Parkdale in Pictures: Its Development to 1889*. Local History Handbook No. 7. Toronto Public Library Board. Toronto: 1991.

Lundell, Liz. *The Estates of Old Toronto*. Boston Mills Press. Erin, Ontario: 1997.

Mackay, Claire. *The Toronto Story*. Annick Press. Toronto: 1990.

Macmillan Dictionary of Canadian Biography. 4th ed. Macmillan. Toronto: 1978.

Martyn, Ethel. "Early History of York Township and Some of the Early Pioneers." 5 March 1934. Typescript in the St. Clair/Dufferin Public Library, Local History Collection.

Martyn, Lucy Booth. *Aristocratic Toronto*. Gage Publishing. Toronto: 1980.

Martyn, Lucy Booth. *Toronto, 100 Years of Grandeur: The Inside Stories of Toronto's Great Homes and the People Who Lived There*. Pagurian Press. Toronto: 1978.

Martyn, Lucy Booth. *A View of Original Toronto: The Fabric of York/Toronto circa 1834*. Paget Press. Sutton West, Ontario: 1983.

McHugh, Patricia. *Toronto Architecture: A City Guide*. 2nd ed. McClelland and Stewart. Toronto: 1989.

McMullin, Stanley E. "Thomas Chandler Haliburton." *Canadian Writers and Their Works*. Fiction Series, Volume 2. Edited by Robert Lecker, Jack David, and Ellen Quigley. Toronto: ECW Press, 1989. 27-76.

Mika, Nick, and Helma Mika. *Place Names in Ontario: Their Name Origins and History*. Mika Publishing. Belleville, Ontario: 1977.

Miles and Company. *Illustrated Historical Atlas of the County of York/selected and reprinted from the original 1878 edition*. P. Martin Associates. Toronto: 1969.

Montcalm, Louis-Joseph. *Journal du marquis de Montcalm durant sa campagnes en Canada de 1756 á 1759*. Edited by Henry Raymond Casgrain. Quebec: 1895.

Moon, Lynda, Barbara Myrvold, and Elizabeth Ridler. *Historical Walking Tour of Lawrence Park*. Revised edition. Toronto Public Library Board. Toronto: 1995.

Myrvold, Barbara. *Historical Walking Tour of the Danforth*. Toronto Public Library Board. Toronto: 1992.

Myrvold, Barbara. *Historical Walking Tour of Kensington Market and College Street*. Toronto Public Library Board. Toronto: 1993.

North Toronto Historical Society. *Davisville Village Walk*. 1984. [typescript]

North Toronto Historical Society. *Eglinton-Pears Park Walk*. Revised edition, 1984. [typescript]

Patterson, Cynthia, Carol McDougall, and George Levin. *Bloor-Dufferin in Pictures*. Local History Handbook No. 5. Toronto Public Library. Toronto: 1986.

Preview Travel Destination Guides: Surrey, Kent and Sussex. <http://www.destinations.previewtravelcom/DestGuides/0,1208,WEB_211,00.html>

Queen's Own Rifles of Canada. *The Rifleman Online: The Queen's Own Rifles of Canada*. <http://www.qor.com>

Rayburn, Alan. *Place Names of Ontario*. University of Toronto Press. Toronto: 1997.

Rempel, J.I. *The Town of Leaside: A Brief History*. East York Historical Society. 1982.

Ritchie, Donald. *North Toronto*. Stoddart Publishing. Toronto: 1992.

Robertson, John Ross. *Landmarks of Toronto: A Collection of Historical Sketches of the Old Town of York from 1792 until 1833, and of Toronto from 1834 to 1914*. Six volumes. Toronto: 1894–1914.

Robinson, Percy J. *Toronto during the French Regime*. Ryerson Press. Toronto: 1933.

Robson, Mary E. *The Origins of Street Names in Toronto's Ward 5*. Community History Project, Spadina Road Library. Toronto: 1987.

Russell, Victor L., ed. *Forging a Consensus: Historical Essays on Toronto*. University of Toronto Press for the Toronto Sesquicentennial Board. Toronto: 1984.

Sauriol, Charles. *Pioneers of the Don*. Charles Sauriol. East York: 1995.

Scadding, Henry. *Toronto of Old*. 2nd ed. Edited by Frederick H. Armstrong. Dundurn Press. Toronto: 1987. First edition published in 1873.

Simcoe, Elizabeth. *The Diary of Mrs. John Graves Simcoe*. Edited by John Ross Robertson. William Briggs. Toronto: 1911.

Steckly, John. "Toronto or is that Taranteau?" Heritage Toronto Homepage. 1999.

A Street Called Front. Marathon Realty. Toronto: 1983.

Toronto Region Architectural Conservancy. *A Study of Rusholme Road*. Toronto: 1991.

Town, Harold. *Albert Franck: Keeper of the Lanes*. Toronto: McClelland and Stewart, 1974.

White, Randall. *Too Good to Be True: Toronto in the 1920s*. Dundurn Press. Toronto: 1993.

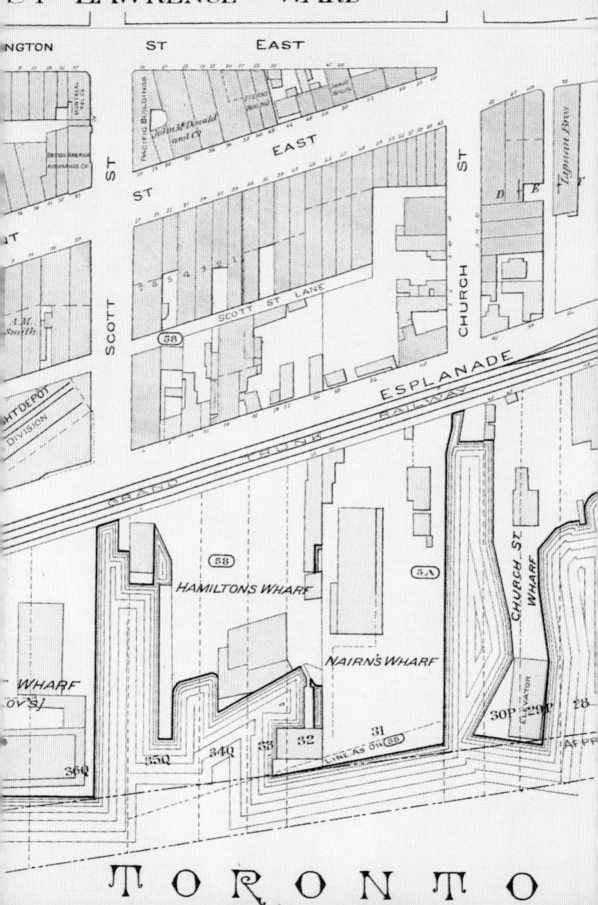

NGTON   ST   EAST

MONTREAL TEL. CO

BRITISH AMERICA ASSURANCE CO

A.M. Smith

PACIFIC BUILDINGS

John McDonald and Co

ST

EAST

ST

SCOTT   ST

SCOTT ST LANE

58

EAST

CHURCH   ST

Tapman Bros

D   E

FREIGHT DEPOT

DIVISION

ESPLANADE

RAILWAY

TRUNK

GRAND

58

HAMILTON'S WHARF

NAIRN'S WHARF

5A

CHURCH ST WHARF

ELEVATOR

WHARF
OV'S.

36Q

35Q   34Q   33   32   31

LINE AS ON 38

30P   29P   28

APP

TORONTO

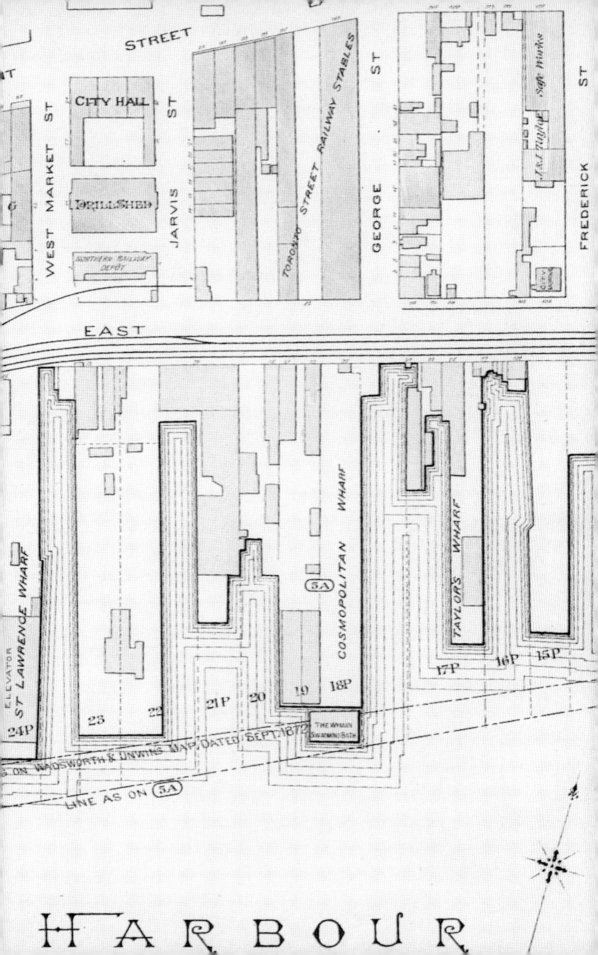